Soul Body Fusion

The Missing Piece
for Healing and Beyond

Soul Body Fusion

The Missing Piece
for Healing and Beyond

Jonette Crowley

**Stone Tree
Publishing**

Soul Body Fusion
StoneTree Publishing
Copyright © 2020 Jonette Crowley

All Rights Reserved. No part of this publication may be reproduced, stored in a retrieval system or transmitted in any form or by any means—electronic, mechanical, photocopying, recording, or otherwise—without prior written permission from the publisher, except for the inclusion of brief quotations in a review.

ISBN # 978-0-5785266-3-8 (Paperback)
978-0-9785384-6-0 (ebook)

Printed in the United States of America

Copyright Page Disclaimer:
This book is not intended in any way to dispense medical advice. Nothing in it should be construed as a replacement for consultation with or treatment from your physician. *Soul Body Fusion* provides information to enhance your personal, emotional, and spiritual well-being. The stories of improvement in health are indicative of the individuals herein represented and do not constitute an implied promise or expectation of outcome.

Soul Body Fusion® is a registered trademark of the
Center for Creative Consciousness. www.JonetteCrowley.com

*Dedicated to all of you,
for your commitment to
growth and to making
this world a better place.*

Contents

Part 1
Why Soul Body Fusion Now?

1. The Missing Piece in Our Potential 3
2. Activating the Earth Elements. 13
3. The Goddess and the Grail Codes 21

Part 2
The Process

4. The Birth of the Soul Body Fusion Process 51
5. Fusing Your Soul 65
6. Doing Soul Body Fusion with Another 91
7. Healing and Healers. 117

Part 3
Going Deeper

8. Science and the Soul 145
9. Other Helpful Ideas for Spiritual Growth 169
10. Resources and Frequently Asked Questions 191
11. More Mysteries Revealed 205
12. A Call to Service 223
Bibliography. 227
Index 229
About the Author 233
Endnotes 235

Acknowledgments

This book was written because so many people took the simple tool of Soul Body Fusion to heart and began using it to change their lives and the health and well-being of those around them. It was their stories that compelled me to teach and write. A huge thank you to them for sharing the experiences and inspiration that are so important in this book! Still, I would have continued to procrastinate but for the impetus of my friend and German-language agent, Wulfing Von Rohr, who sold the book idea to Random House.

My professional and loving editor, Margaret Harrell, was always there when I needed her. She made the solo job of a writer become a partnership. Special thanks to those friends who read the manuscript and added their wisdom: Nancy Oberman, Jarla Ahlers, Berdine de Visser, Jim Dunne, Nadja Nicholl. None of this could have happened without the support of my office manager, Lisa Smith, and personal assistant, Ev Luceris Davidson. My husband, Ed Oakley, himself an author, was tolerant of all the time I spent writing. His encouragement and love are mainstays in my journey.

Thanks also to those European publishers who are bringing Soul Body Fusion to their readers in Norway, Sweden, Finland, and the Netherlands.

The greatest acknowledgment goes to you, the reader. You are the ones who believe that miraculous change can be simple.

Author's Note

I've learned a lot from my spirit guides over the past twenty years.

I have a great life, fabulous work, good health, wonderful family and friends... Who would have thought that there was still a missing piece and it was right under my nose? Sure, I can channel for folks, lead people to multidimensional states of consciousness, and open energetic portals at power places. But a little process of aligning body and soul is proving to be so unexpectedly powerful... and so easy to learn.

White Eagle, my main spirit guide, pushed me to teach Soul Body Fusion. Before that it was just another spiritual tool I used for myself. My more cosmic guide, Mark, who doesn't *ever* care about such earthly things, told me the name—Soul Body Fusion—and to trademark it. That was my first hint that I had entered a game with a grander plan than I could foresee.

I still have all those great things ... and something else... a greater version of me.

This book is the next step in the unfolding of an invisible game plan. Only now, *you* are on the team too!

July, 2011
Denver, Colorado

PART I

Why Soul Body Fusion Now?

There is some kiss we want with our whole lives, the touch of spirit on the body.

-Rumi

Chapter 1

The Missing Piece in Our Potential

> *Humans are big on choosing what you want to see after the transformation, but in this transformation you don't even have to choose the outcome, because the outcome is impossible to choose from the limitation of you as a chooser.*
>
> -Mark

Alienated from Our Highest Self

We each have a beautiful soul but are sometimes unable to bring it fully into our physical body. We live our lives with our lights half on, unable to magnetize the health, wealth, and well-being that is our birthright. The frequency of our souls and the frequency of our bodies are, more often than not, misaligned. We might experience resistance between the two, or outright conflict and disassociation. This occurs because of life's traumas, pain, disappointments, and grief. We stumble along without the full power and presence of our spirit. In many ways we have lost the energy keys that can allow full fusion of our divinity into our humanity.

Do you feel that your spirit and body aren't in tune? Do you sometimes feel ungrounded or like you don't belong? Do you *know* that you should have more energy and better health but can't get there? Imagine how it will feel to have the light of your spirit fully and permanently joined in your body, as they are meant to be.

Elephants, following an instinct, head for the hills before a tsunami hits. Birds fly south for the winter. Salmon return to the exact stream of their birth to spawn. But humans… well… we are largely disassociated from our natural instincts. We seem to be the only species that continually makes choices counter to its own health.

For the past few hundred years, western scientific philosophies have cleaved a separation between spirit and matter. Spirit—that immeasurable, illogical force—was discounted and handed over to religions, while matter was dissected and studied, becoming the only reality. Duality was king. Not only was our spirit severed from our physicality, but our intrinsic divinity was denied. When our religions put God outside us, the separation became solidified. In the process of material survival we've identified with our flesh and lost our soul, our essence. Simply put, we've become alienated from our essence.

Feeling the loss of our spirit—and with it our innate power—some of us try to reach it through meditation and spiritual practices. Others might become numb from overwork or addictions. But here is the fallacy: often we are chasing our soul by leaving our body behind. This has certainly been true for me. I've been seeking peace and enlightenment by learning to go to higher and higher spaces. I had lovely transcendent experiences, but I couldn't always bring the feelings back to my body or integrate them into my life. I was ungrounded and didn't even know it! I remember back in my college days a group of guys called me "Space Queen." I was a good student; I had an active social life. What did they see that I didn't?

In the current environment of separation, some tend to pursue spiritual goals, but in the process discount the value of earthly life. Have you ever heard someone claim, "This is my last life; after this I'm out of here?" What does this say about how we value our lives? The message is, life on Earth is some sort of karmic prison sentence and we can't wait to be done with it. Maybe, just maybe, we've got it all backward. Instead of leaving our bodies behind, perhaps the *first step* in spiritual growth and physical or emotional well-being is to bring spirit back fully into the body. We need to *begin* by being whole. After all, we can only change something to the extent we are part of it.

Reclaiming Our Wholeness

The Soul Body Fusion technique makes the connection with our potential more alive and clear. When we bring our consciousness into our body, our uniqueness is radiated into our life, relationships and surroundings.

Glenda Green, author of *Love Without End*, summarizes it this way: "The Soul is crying for a reality experience which only physical life can give to it. The body is crying for an immortal experience which only the soul can give to it. As you permit this union to fulfill itself, you will directly know what it feels like to be the love that you are."[1]

When more of our spirit is merged into our cells, an undeniable shift is created. It becomes the starting point for a new reality where health, happiness, abundance, and meaning are supported from the highest realms. With Soul Body Fusion our wholeness isn't so much achieved as remembered.

By fully harmonizing with your higher aspects—which I call soul—you are opening the door for the limited, three-dimensional you to experience greater realities beyond time and space. Events are brought about that may look quite miraculous to the small self. Changes that, from a purely physical standpoint, seem impossible or take enormous effort or time can be instantaneous when your greater self is available for the task. When your soul and body are operating as a unified whole, there is no lack. As a whole, you are a sovereign, creative force. Your own soul may be the missing piece in your potential. Accessing your vast talents is what makes the Soul Body Fusion process so powerful, with sometimes spectacular results.

Some Results[1]

Just to give you a taste of what you will learn as you read about and practice the tools in these chapters, here are quotes from people who have experienced Soul Body Fusion:

- The most graceful, easy, beautiful way to enlightenment—my soul is home and the struggle is over. I'm ecstatic!
- It is the first time in my life I've felt real happiness.
- I was diagnosed with Type 2 diabetes and took medication three times a day. After the first Fusion I scaled back on my drugs. I believe SBF has fixed my body so it produces insulin normally again. I was just at the doctor's, and he confirmed I no longer have diabetes! I cannot find another explanation for this except Soul Body Fusion.

---

[1] Throughout this book, examples of healing are individuals' reported experiences only. The author makes no medical or curative claims for Soul Body Fusion.

- I gave SBF to "D," who had melanoma in her eye and metastases throughout her body. Doctors said there was barely any chance of curing her except by chemotherapy. The understanding she received in the Fusion about her childhood had a critical impact on her health. Her test results improved, and chemotherapy wasn't needed. The metastases in her body have completely disappeared.

- I was depressed, jealous, angry, and isolated. I didn't trust myself or anyone else. In the Fusion session I got my soul grounded and all the energy changed! I had a 180-degree shift immediately! Even my boyfriend changed. He didn't know what happened. It is now easy for me to control myself and focus again. I finally broke out of the box and am free to be the real Jenny!

Although in some cases the Soul Body Fusion process results in healing, it is more than a healing tool. It expands you and your potential at all levels. One woman told me, "The lid is off. What was impossible before happens easily now." It may bring you understanding, clarity, greater access to wisdom, more self-love, accelerated personal growth, more spiritual gifts… It puts you on the road to what I call "uncaused well-being."

We have trillions of cells in our body and they all respond to vibration—light, sound, energy, love. Our soul is the highest vibration we can hold, encompassing our very greatest light and potential. When we consciously invoke our soul to permanently harmonize and merge with our physicality, our cells change. Deepak Chopra, MD, says it this way: "Everything the soul does is translated into a process in the body. You literally cannot have a body without the soul. This is the forgotten miracle. Each of us is a soul made flesh."[2]

Getting Your Spirit Back in Your Life

Soul Body Fusion is a simple process you can do on yourself and others that realigns the body at a cellular level with the highest possible spirit or light it can hold. The changes are permanent and never-ending—permanent in that when your cells change to harmonize with your higher aspects they will remain at that lighter frequency. The change is never-ending in that there is no limit to your soul. Soul Body Fusion begets an interactive process in which the soul stimulates the cells to harmonize at ever-higher frequencies. In this way it is an evolutionary catalyst, opening doorways of accelerating growth. It is a powerful tool for creating new realities here and now. Stefan, an SBF Certified Teacher in Bulgaria, explains it this way: "'You reap what you sow;' in other words, we attract people and events that resonate with our vibrations. It is similar to how a radio works. There is a small generator inside the radio that sends out waves with a desired frequency. These waves resonate with those in the ether and then the antenna receives the resonant vibrations. It is the same with us. We emit a vibration whose resonance brings us the corresponding program. The main question is: 'What am I tuning to—the higher me? Or mass consciousness?' With Soul Body Fusion we change the modulation from very poor quality to the very best quality and we are able to consciously choose our desired programs of life. With the ability to hold and emit higher frequencies, we create new realities for ourselves." This process follows a spiritual law that higher frequencies, because they contain more energy, trump lower frequencies. In other words, consciousness always moves in a higher, upward direction.

Although I speak of fusing our soul and body and say that our soul "comes into" our cells, it doesn't mean we've been living a soulless existence. Our soul has endless higher frequencies of itself with which we haven't been in touch. The Fusion process aligns our current self—no matter how high we already are—with the even finer, lighter, more cosmic aspects of our soul. The more of our soul we embody, the greater ability we have to reach even higher. Just as the efficiency of a computer and the sophistication of the programs it can run depend on its operating system, our access to the wisdom of the universe has been limited by our mainly three-dimensional system for operating.

Valerie Hunt, Professor Emeritus of Biological Science at UCLA, author of *Infinite Mind—Science of the Human Vibrations of Consciousness*, has been researching the science of human vibrations for decades. She noticed that there is a scale of frequencies that corresponds to a person's level of development and state of mind. She found that the normal frequency for a materialistic person is in the neighborhood of 250 Hertz. (Hertz is defined as the number of cycles per second. A higher number indicates a wave with a higher frequency and thus more energy.) Healers are in the 400 to 800 Hz range, while those with "psychic gifts" have vibrations in the range of 800 to 900 Hz. People she described as having "mystical personalities" exhibit frequencies of over 900Hz.[3] We can imagine that bringing in more of our soul is increasing our vibrational field, opening up spiritual and healing doors that remain shut to those with lower and slower energetic fields.

For most of us our biology hasn't been programmed to hold the higher self. Even when we succeed in having a transcendent spiritual moment, the feeling can't be sustained. The Soul Body Fusion process changes your body so that you can hold more power and access dimensions that were inaccessible before. Generally we've been able to reach these high dimensions only through spiritual practices—in essence, leaving our body behind and traveling with our consciousness. In so doing, we're maintaining the duality between spirit and matter. Now is the time to finally experience our wholeness. With this we get a totally new operating system on which to run marvelous and magical programs of life.

An Unpredictable Transformation

It is impossible to predict the impact of Soul Body Fusion on an individual. We can't know what gifts will be offered until we take the next step. I am reminded of an old joke that still makes me smile: Two caterpillars are sitting on a leaf when a butterfly zooms by, startling them. One turns to the other and says, "Boy, you'll never get me up in one of those things."

In this new way of being, our futures will be determined by what we truly are and what we can be, not by what and where we've been—allowing for the emergence of unmanifested potential. In short, Soul Body Fusion makes it easier to be the unique and wonderful being you are! Think of your soul as a continual source of support, wisdom, and nurturing. The more it is integrated, the more your life flows.

These times are about combining light and matter, fusing soul and body, bringing together the energies of the ancient Solar Discs and the Grail Codes. It is a time to be illuminated. We can all feel the urgency today for personal and global transformation. We spend more money on more things and are less healthy and less happy. Our paradigm of conflict and exploitation rather than cooperation is burdening our Earth. We yearn for a more holistic world view. These are unprecedented times with unprecedented opportunities. We are leaders in consciousness evolution—figuring out new rules of the game… or is it a whole new game?

This is a practical handbook that provides clear instructions, numerous examples, and the mystical and scientific background—everything you need to do Fusions on yourself and others. I invite you to step with me into the magical adventures that led to my discovery of Soul Body Fusion. It is a journey of hope, healing, and wholeness. This book carries energies for awakening. Soul Body Fusion is a gift to you and all whom you will touch.

Chapter 2

Activating the Earth Elements

Jonette is no ordinary spiritual being. I saw a spiritual leader even before she told me of her life's journey. Jonette is a wise grandmother in a youthful personage. She is a chosen one—to awaken, teach, and guide us on our true path of walking forward in the future world.

-Grand Chief Woableza,
Council of Native Spiritual Elders

A Spiritual Indiana Jones

Like all discoveries of significance that come in a flash of insight, the prelude takes considerable preparation. For Soul Body Fusion, the preparatory work occupied five years, encompassed four continents, and included lots of hiking.

Although my professional career is as a leadership consultant, my passion is exploration. For over twenty years I have received clear and conscious guidance from two spirit teachers. White Eagle is a Master who works with people directly through readings and healing. Mark is a cosmic magnetic presence, not from the physical realms at all. He focuses on teaching skills in the higher dimensions of quantum consciousness through classes and workshops. They are part of the White Brotherhood, a collective of Masters and guides whose focus is the spiritual evolution of humanity. Both guides tell me where to go, but only if I ask.

As an explorer in the outer world, I am a traveler to the core, traipsing to over sixty countries and counting. I love to visit power places and sacred spots, usually taking along fellow spiritual travelers. We open to insights and look for hidden energies or ancient keys. Along the way I've gained skills as a modern shaman. With help from my spirit guides, I am adept at navigating through eighth dimensional consciousness and bringing others along for the ride. At every step we've acquired understanding and undergone transformation, often beyond words. I am an unconventional shaman in that I'm not a student of any particular native lineage or culture; therefore, the rituals and belief systems built up over the ages don't limit me. Information comes from my inner guides, while energies and initiations come directly from the Earth and beyond. The benefit of this is that I can be flexible and pragmatic, always looking for what works with the minimum of rules. My ultimate goal is to assist in the transformation of the human experience by exploring, then creating pathways to higher consciousness.

Just as our cells need to be readied to hold more of our higher dimensional essence, so does Mother Earth need to be cleared and prepared for her dimensional shifts. At four power places around the globe I've led groups to activate, one by one, each of the elements: earth, water, fire, and air. The completed activations became the prerequisite for Soul Body Fusion—the bigger picture, only seen in retrospect.

Nepal: Activating the Element of Earth

In 2003, the Himalayan kingdom of Nepal beckoned me and thirteen hardy adventurers to hike for fourteen days to the Mt. Everest base camp, at over eighteen thousand feet in altitude. Besides the daunting physical challenge, we sought to connect with the nature-inspired Buddhism of the region. Before flying off to Kathmandu, I asked White Eagle what our spiritual mission was. He explained that the Earth, in order to protect humanity, had stored the negative energy that humans have created over the centuries in a safe and remote place—at the root of the Himalayas. Our mission was to use the Light and the power of good to begin to release the darkness stored there. This would help free the planet from its negative burden. I've learned that I don't need to understand these spiritual missions or even rationally believe them. I simply show up with the right intention, trust, and follow my instincts. Really, that is the best any of us can do.

Our work did help cleanse the Earth of stored toxic energy. This allowed the further opening of an energetic gateway in a nearby mountain—Ama Dablam—one of the world's five most magnificent peaks. From there, sweet, strong energies continue to pour through the Earth's meridians. Our gift from this is what I call the Himalayan Heart Activation. It is a transfer of power and connection that can ignite your heart like an electrical charge. (I'll share with you how to do this activation in Chapter 9: Other Helpful Ideas for Spiritual Growth.) Our meditations and prayers during the spectacular journey in the Himalayas activated the element of earth.

Peru: Activating the Element of Water

A year following our sojourn in Nepal, many of the same travelers joined me on a spiritual adventure to Peru: the Amazon River; Lake Titicaca; and the Inca Trail, which we hiked to Machu Picchu—a mystical, terraced citadel in the clouds. According to White Eagle, one of our missions was to connect with the spirit of water in the Amazon, asking to heal the water element throughout the world. We did this in a magical meditation as we floated in a canoe down a tributary of the Madre de Dios River at dusk.

In addition to our work with water I had my own mission. Ever since reading *The Secret of the Andes*, I wanted to learn more about the mysterious Sun Disc of Lemuria. According to the book and some Native American legends, prior to the cataclysmic sinking of the great Pacific civilization called Lemuria, some of the sacred scrolls containing records of the universe were brought by a Lemurian master teacher named Amaru Muru to the Andes for safekeeping. The most precious of these items was an enormous disc of gold containing encoded knowledge, that functioned as a cosmic computer. The sun disc, or solar disc, was taken to a hidden monastery near Lake Titicaca, where it was protected by the Incan priesthood. The legend was captivating, and the adventurous part of me was hoping to be led to the secret sun disc. Why not? I got what I wanted, but not at all in the way that I expected. It happened during an evening meditation in Cuzco, led by our Andean shaman Mallku. I found myself on an inner spiritual journey that was as clear as the room around me. In front of me was a flat-topped pyramid, resembling those constructed by the Mayans and Incas. I somehow knew that to enter, I had to ask permission of an unseen guardian. After the third time I asked, "Who guards this place?" a brown-skinned Mayan-looking god, wearing a feathered cape appeared. The guardian of the inner sanctum was the Great Initiator—known as Quetzalcoatl to the Aztecs, Kulkulcan to the Mayans. His feathers identified him as the "plumed serpent," sometimes called the "Rainbow Serpent." In nearly every culture that has inner initiation rites, the feathered serpent, under different names, guards the doorway of wisdom, testing to find whether the journeyer is ready and worthy. He only appears at the highest initiations and is sometimes seen as a dragon. One cannot ask for such an initiation. It is given when all is ready. I passed the test that night by innately knowing that I must ask permission of the guardian and continue asking three times, until he appeared.

Using my soul name, "Kumara," I requested admittance into the pyramid. The guardian moved aside. Instantly, my vision changed. I was alone inside the pyramid, ascending up seven luminous steps leading to the top platform, where a massive golden sun disc radiated endless light and power. The energy hit me physically like packets of geometrically coded information shooting out from the sun disc into my cells. The reality of the energetic downloads caused my body to shake, shudder, and heat up. Some of the other meditators opened their eyes in concern as I shook and swayed. It felt as if I was being deeply reprogrammed with cryptic codes embedded into my very being—the Sun Disc Codes.

This is how I received my solar initiation, directly and spontaneously from the higher worlds. Having accepted the energetic codes into my being, I can transfer parts of the solar initiation to others. It is my belief that when I or any of us receives higher energy, knowledge, or spiritual initiations, these gifts become embedded and strengthened in the whole fabric of human consciousness. They are thus made available to anyone who can connect to them. It is as if, through us, the higher wisdom is transformed or repackaged in a format that can now be widely accessible to the rest of humanity. This is what is occurring with the Sun Disc Codes and solar initiations. For perhaps thousands of years this knowledge has been lost to us, hidden until we were ready to claim it.

You may want to read the detailed story of these two journeys, to the Himalayas and the Andes, in my book *The Eagle and the Condor: A True Story of an Unexpected Mystical Journey*. Readers have reported experiencing the energies of initiation directly. The book's name comes from an ancient native legend that states: "When the eagle of North America and the condor of South America unite, the spirit of peace will awaken on Earth." Many believe that time is now.

Mt. Kilimanjaro: Activating the Element of Fire

During a profound meditation in 1989, just moments before I channeled White Eagle for the first time, I was shown a vision of an energetic reawakening of Africa: A towering crystal as big as a skyscraper was perched on top of a mountain, sending brilliant, transformational light out to Africa and the world. Deep in my soul the seed was planted. I knew that the mountain was Kilimanjaro in Tanzania, and someday I would climb it and carry with me a symbolic quartz crystal. It was clear to me that for the world to get to its next level of enlightenment, the rich power of Africa needed to be awakened. Now, in 2011, we watch as people in North Africa and the Middle East seek to reclaim their rights from despotic regimes.

Mt. Kilimanjaro, whose summit sits above the equatorial clouds at 19,340 feet, is the highest point in Africa, and the world's highest freestanding volcano. Fire is the element of transformation and transfiguration. For seven days in February

2006, our group of spiritual adventurers hiked the Machame Trail to Uhuru Peak—Kili's summit. The ascension was steep, the gain in altitude literally dizzying. I have been to the top of Mt. Kalapathar in the Himalayas, hiked the high passes on the Inca Trail, and summited fifteen of Colorado's highest peaks, but this time the altitude gain proved too much for me. For three days, suffering from acute mountain sickness, I stumbled up the mammoth mountain. I couldn't keep food, water, or medication down. My head was racked with thousands of stabbing swords. My brain tissue and lungs filled with fluid—cerebral and pulmonary edema. The capillaries in my face began to burst, giving me the appearance of black eyes. That was it. Willpower and grit couldn't get me another step. I had made it to the summit base camp Barafu at 15,000 feet. I collapsed in our tent, while my husband Ed, using the satellite phone, woke up friends and healers in Denver to pray for me. On the evening of the full moon, I handed Ed the crystal that I had brought from Peru, for him and the others to take to the top of Africa.

There is not enough gratitude in my heart to thank Ed and our fellow hikers, many of whom were sick too, for helping me those last three horrible days. I also believe that the groups of friends in the United States and Europe who were holding the space for our spiritual mission were vital to its success.

The mountain had taken so much from all of us. Out of twelve fit and eager hikers who began the journey, only four made it to the top; two others made it close. What did it give us? Fire makes dough into bread, clay into a pot, molten metal into steel. It transforms our essence into something strong and entirely different than before. The Himalayas gave us the Heart Activation. The Andes activated the Sun Disc's Codes of wisdom. Kilimanjaro gave us fire in our bellies so we would know our own strength.

Activating the Element of Air

Several months out of Africa I allowed myself the luxury of an easy trip—to England to visit Glastonbury and Stonehenge, and hopefully to see some crop circles. I went with three Dutch women with whom I have developed a close sisterhood. We sought to experience the famed energies of Avalon. But none of us sensed much. Disappointed, we asked White Eagle, "Why?" I channeled that the energies of power spots are moving and changing. Different places are becoming powerful. As we humans open up we are actually becoming movable power vortices ourselves.

Having led groups to mountains in Asia, South America, and Africa to activate the elements of earth, water, and fire respectively, I asked White Eagle where to go to activate the element of air. I was pretty sure it had to be at sea level, since from experience I *knew* there just isn't any air on top of a mountain!

The four of us sat in our cozy English farmhouse, discussing where we thought air would be activated. Elizabeth thought a Greek island would be nice. I was pulling for Hawaii. When we asked White Eagle, his answer was simple and completely unexpected: "Malta."

"Malta?" I thought. "That certainly wasn't on *my* short list of places to visit."

Berdine saved the day, as she knew something about Malta. She informed the rest of us that this island nation near the southern coast of Italy has some of the oldest temples on Earth and a strong ancient culture of reverence for the goddess. Our journey to Malta gave us the opening that would lead to Soul Body Fusion.

Chapter 3

The Goddess and the Grail Codes: Awakening our DNA

You are to awaken the Grail Codes. They are the other half of the Sun Disc Codes that you uncovered in the Andes. Together they form a new foundation for human consciousness that is halfway between the current state and the state of enlightenment. The Grail Codes are latent in everyone and need to be awakened when the consciousness of a person is ready.

-Mark

Preparing for the Journey

These words, received from my spirit guide Mark in 2007, outlined the spiritual mission for the last segment of the five-year odyssey that has taken me to the Mount Everest base camp, the Amazon and the Andes, the top of Mount Kilimanjaro, and finally to the island nation of Malta.

May 2007 was the date for our trip to Malta to activate the element of air, or wind, for the planet. I had just published *The Eagle and the Condor* and looked forward to an easier adventure: no mountains to climb, no strange diseases, nice hotels, good food, Mediterranean springtime weather, English speaking.

Under the surface, something big was stirring:

- A Maltese spiritual historian happened to tune in to our upcoming tour through my website. He emailed my organizer: "This group is going to awaken energies that have been dormant on Malta for thousands of years." He also told her that the wind was an important element in the ceremonies of the prehistoric people on the islands.

- For some reason, the term "Grail Codes" was coming up in my reading—from many varied sources.

- The topic of dragons likewise kept popping up, certainly not a subject in which I had any interest.

- My flying dreams became more prevalent and clear, especially one in which I was stuck inside a gigantic dome, unable to move through the ceiling—as I normally can in such dreams. I vowed to keep a lookout for this dome, certain that I would recognize it.

A week before flying to Malta, I taught a workshop in Norway. One evening, as four of us overlooked the Oslo fjord from my friend Siri's sitting room, we called in my spirit guide Mark to do a channel. The purpose was to help me prepare for the trip. Anne-Lise asked the questions I suggested as Bjorn scribbled notes.

We asked what our group needed to do to activate the element of air. Mark answered that we would know the time and place and how to do it. Can I admit right here that I hate that kind of answer from the guides? Why can't they just tell me what to do? My performance anxiety went way up; after all, forty people were paying to do this trip with me. As I channeled, Anne-Lise asked Mark: "What else does Jonette and her group need to do as part of their spiritual mission on Malta?"

"She is to awaken the Grail Codes," Mark channeled through me.

"What are the Grail Codes?" was clearly the next question.

> *The Grail Codes are the other half of the Sun Disc Codes that she uncovered in Peru. Together they form a new foundation for human consciousness that is halfway between the current state and the state of enlightenment. The Grail Codes are latent in everyone and need to be awakened when the consciousness of a person is ready. Jonette is one of only three people on the planet who can do this.*

I was surprised at that last part; however, I assumed this is because I carry the Sun Disc Codes from the initiation in Peru three years earlier. I shared this tidbit on the phone with Ed, who was still in Colorado. Being sort of a smart aleck, he queried, "Did you ask who the other two people are?" He is always there to make sure I don't get too self-important.

Our last question to Mark that evening was "Tell us more about the role of dragons, since Jonette keeps thinking about them."

> *Dragons have been feared throughout time, not for who they are but for what they protect. They are the guardians of the doors to wisdom and knowledge. If you meet a dragon on an inner journey, you are always alone and so is the dragon. You will be tested. If you pass the test, the doorway will open to you and the*

dragon will be your friend. The gates are only open to those who have no fear of the dragon.

We discussed the symbolism of the dragon guarding the doors of knowledge. "Isn't the serpent the same thing?" we pondered. For example, it was the serpent that guarded the tree of knowledge of good and evil in the biblical Garden of Eden. He tested Eve by offering her the forbidden fruit. Did humanity metaphorically fall from paradise because we failed the test, not ready to hold the power and responsibility of wisdom? I recalled that it was the god form of the feathered serpent that guarded the pyramid of the sun disc, where I received the codes of awakening on my inner journey in Peru.

Magical Malta

The crucial location of Malta, in the center of the Mediterranean Sea, has made it a strategic crossroads from the very beginning of history. Comprised of three tiny islands—Malta, Gozo, and Camino—it has been home to prehistoric temple builders, Phoenicians, Greeks, Sicilians, Romans, Byzantines, Arabs, and Normans. It was invaded by Turks, the waters besieged by pirates. St. Paul was shipwrecked on its shores, and the crusading Knights of St. John of Jerusalem settled there. Napoleon captured Malta in 1798, surrendering it to the British two years later. Malta, now part of the European Union, gained its independence in 1964. Its immense prehistoric temple complexes are said to be older than Stonehenge or the Giza pyramids of Egypt. This is a sacred place, where the goddess has been worshiped from ancient times.

Our initial day of touring brought us to the town of Mosta in central Malta to see the magnificent rotunda of the Church of the Assumption of Our Lady. Three things impressed me about the church:

- First, it is beautiful! It has the third largest unsupported dome in the world, after St. Peter's Basilica in the Vatican and St. Sophia in Istanbul. To design a Catholic church with a rotunda rather than the traditional cruciform layout was revolutionary in the mid-1800s. In terms of sacred architecture, domes have often designated the power of the feminine. In fact, the bishop at the time of the construction considered a dome to be pagan, not Christian, and he wasn't too pleased with the design. However, the parishioners overruled him, and Mosta would have its extraordinary domed church. A previous church from 1614 sat on this location, but who knows about the more ancient past? I believe that the famed Maltese architect Giorgio Gronget de Vasse, who designed the church with its impressive dome, was a true visionary. His own research led him to be among the first with the idea that Malta was a remnant of Atlantis. Perhaps he had the feeling that the church he was building stood over ancient Atlantean holy ground, and that his design needed to match the grand essence of the place.

- Second, in 1942 during World War II, a German bomb pierced the dome… but failed to explode! This has become quite the local legendary event, leading some to claim the Mosta Dome miracle. This helped confirm to me that the church stood on powerfully protected holy ground.

- Third, as soon as I walked into the church and looked up, I recognized the spectacular pattern in the rotunda! It was the very dome through which I could not penetrate in my flying dream some weeks earlier. Since my spirit can always pass through ordinary buildings, the fact that I could not get through the domed ceiling in my dream indicates that it was sealed with a spiritual protection. What was it protecting?

Our group took turns standing on the center of the magnificent church, enjoying the powerful energies. For Evalyn, a doctor from the Netherlands, it was a very special spot. Her inner senses opened up, and as she described to me later, she could "see" dragons leaving from the basement out through the dome. Evidently, one dragon thought it curious that someone could sense this and he telepathically informed Evalyn, "You have some strange friends." Imagine, an invisible dragon calling us strange! What was especially interesting about this was that she had no idea that my guide had told me that dragons guard the portals to wisdom. Later that evening, White Eagle channeled more information about Evalyn's experience with the dragons at the Mosta Dome:

> *When the dragons are seen and recognized, it means you've attained a certain level of consciousness and you are allowed to proceed. Since you are part of this group's consciousness, you did this in service to the group. The group's high awareness when visiting the dome today released a cork that has been holding back an infusion of wisdom, codes, light, history... the future. The dragons, in seeing you and being recognized by you, gave your group clearance to pass through the portal, to remove the stopper... We do not know yet if your group can call awake the Grail Codes, which is the awakening of the Goddess, although the opportunity is there. You have the power.*

During our first evening in Malta we had the good fortune to meet researchers Dagmar Claire and Hubert Zeitlmair, h.c.D. Based in Germany, they have created the Malta Discovery Prehistory Research Foundation. Their search for evidence of Atlantis brought them to the islands of Malta, which they believe were the administrative center of a large and advanced Ice Age culture, now collectively known as Atlantis. Over dinner they shared some of the fascinating highlights of their findings and, unbeknownst to me at the time, gave me information that pushed me closer to our spiritual mission of awakening the Grail Codes. I learned much more about the secrets of Malta and Atlantis in subsequent interviews with Dr. Hubert Zeitlmair and pouring through their extensive website, www.MaltaDiscovery.org.

The antediluvian, or pre-Flood, history of Malta has been enigmatic ever since the unearthing in the early nineteenth century of a series of thirty-six megalithic sandstone structures, older than any others in Europe. Because of massive Earth changes over thousands of years, some of these temples now rest sunken in the sea surrounding the remaining three Maltese islands. The Zeitlmairs noticed that if you consider all thirty-six structures and their locations as a whole, rather than as independent edifices, they represent a stone-circle system that follows celestial cycles. The pattern reveals that the buildings are laid out in alignment with the rising sun on the spring and autumn equinox. Due to the precession of the equinox—the tilt of the Earth that over time causes a movement in the sun's rising position—the ancient astronomers needed to build new observatory temples every 1,080 years or so. Since it takes 25,920 years for the precession to come full circle, it became clear to the Zeitlmairs (based on the number and location of the ancient stone structures on and around the islands) that people here have been building temples to follow the sun for at least two full precession cycles of 25,920 years each… or for more than 51,840 years! To put this into perspective, the time of the great pharaohs in Egypt was only 5,000 years ago.

Ancient Tablets of Stone

While conducting field research at Malta's megalithic sites, Dagmar and Hubert discovered strange script carved into the stone. The language is older than Sumerian, older than Egyptian hieroglyphics. It turns out to be the syllabaric writing of an archaic (non-Vedic) Sanskrit, sometimes referred to as proto-Sanskrit. Similar writing has been found engraved in stones in Glozel, southern France; in Calabria, southern Italy; in Colombia, South America; on Easter Island; and even in Illinois in the United States. The same script, but on clay tablets has been found in what once was Sumeria and Mesopotamia. Because of the consistency of the proto-Sanskrit symbols widely scattered around the world, the Zeitlmairs presume that it is the ancient Atlantean language; that this was the worldwide language used before the legendary downfall of the Tower of Babel. According to them, later civilizations—such as Sumerians, Akkadians, Egyptians, Babylonians, Assyrians, Phoenicians, Indians, Maya, and Indo-Europeans—have incorporated some of this ancient Sanskrit as a component of their language.

In 1994, German linguist Kurt Schildmann succeeded in finally deciphering this archaic Sanskrit from stone carvings referred to as the Indus Valley texts. (The Indus Valley culture was a Bronze Age civilization in what is now mostly Pakistan, and bits of India and Afghanistan.) This breakthrough enabled the deciphering of similar pre-Flood stone engravings found in Malta and around the world.

As I spoke with Hubert and Dagmar Zeitlmair in the rather noisy Maltese restaurant, Hubert asked me to put out my hand. In it he placed a palm-sized, shiny, smooth black stone with unusual symbols carved into it. My eyes lit up. Excited, I thought I was holding an actual Atlantean artifact from Malta! "Is this from here?" I asked, caressing the stone and the strange glyphs.

"No," came Zeitlmair's surprising reply. "It's from a cave in the United States, a place known as Burrows Cave in Illinois." I was flabbergasted. Who could have imagined that much of what has been discovered about Atlantis and the prehistory of Malta wasn't found in Malta at all, but in a little-known cave in southern Illinois? An intriguing world of ancient secrets opened up for me when I later googled "Burrows Cave."

In 1982, Russell Burrows, a retired Army Brigadier General and experienced caver, happened upon a cave well hidden along a tributary of the Little Wabash River in southern Illinois. In spite of a walled-up entrance and nine feet of silt, Burrows excavated and found large quantities of startling artifacts. He wrote, "I did not have to be a genius to figure out that I stumbled into something that just should not be in Illinois." From the five-hundred-foot tunnel and adjacent chambers he unearthed twelve burial crypts, a golden sarcophagus, urns, grave furniture, weapons, Egyptian-looking inscriptions in gold, and more than four thousand black stone tablets carved with writing, faces, ships, symbols, and maps! I had held one of the stones from this incredible cache. Because of the consistency of the stones and the workmanship of the tablets, the Zeitlmairs believe that Burrows Cave is a library with texts, maps, and figures compiled and copied from much older sources.[4]

This fantastic find is not without precedent. Zeitlmair wrote that a similar coin like object engraved with the same strange signs was found from drilling a well bore in Marshall

County, Illinois. It was reportedly at a depth of one hundred fourteen feet. According to the State Geological Survey in Illinois, the deposits containing the coin are between 200,000 and 400,000 years old! (For more information about other unusual pre-Columbian finds in North America, read David H. Childress's book *Lost Cities of North & Central America*.)

The linguistic breakthrough that Kurt Schildmann made in translating archaic Sanskrit was the missing key in deciphering many of the stone tablets found in Burrows Cave. Hubert Zeitlmair studied with Schildmann; between them they have translated more than one hundred fifty stone tablets from the Illinois find. It is the incredible information carved on these slabs that has formed the basis of the Zeitlmairs' theories about Atlantis and the ancient history of Malta. (For details, please refer to www.MaltaDiscovery.org). All of this becomes woven into the awakening that forms the mystical foundation for Soul Body Fusion.

The Sleeping Goddess

My favorite temple in all of Malta is known as the Hypogeum—literally under the earth. It is the world's only prehistoric underground temple. It eluded discovery until 1902, when workers were digging a cistern for a housing development. It is now a UNESCO World Heritage Site. The spaces are small; only eighty people a day can visit and then only in small groups. Hewn out of the honey-colored sandstone, its curving lines and domed chambers have a distinctly feminine beauty. It is a sound chamber and a place to connect to the oracle. Although the Hypogeum was constructed underground, I saw no signs of fire or soot from burning lamps. My impression was that this was a magical place where the ancient worshipers had harnessed another type of light. More than at any of the other sacred sites in my journeys, the feeling here is surreal, otherworldly—as if by walking in we became gods and goddesses too.

The main chamber in the Hypogeum, Paola, Malta (fig. 3.1)

It was in the main chamber of the Hypogeum that small statuettes of a fat, sleeping lady were found. Archeologists called them fertility symbols. We saw the most famous of these in the Museum of Archeology in the Maltese capital city of Valetta. Only about eight inches long, she is beautifully carved out of sandstone. Sometimes you can look at an artifact and appreciate its historical significance or artistry, but for many in our group this diminutive statue of a corpulent, fully clothed woman touched our hearts. We couldn't take our eyes off her. Some modern spiritual researchers, including Hubert and Dagmar Zeitlmair and Francis Aloisio, a Maltese native who authored the book *Islands of Dreams: The Temples of Malta, Hidden Mysteries Revealed*, believe she symbolizes Ashtatara—a legendary sleeping goddess known also as the Queen of Atlantis.

The Sleeping Goddess Statue
(Photo taken by Jonette through the display case. fig. 3.2)

In a nearby display case was a related but unusual carved piece. We would have glossed over it, except Francis Aloisio, whom we had engaged as our guide, stopped us. The carving was of a pallet, similar in size and shape to the one on which the sleeping goddess reclined. However, this had no goddess, only a cover that might be used to drape over a dead body. On it was ancient writing that Dr. Zeitlmair deciphered: "Here rests the head—the Commodore of the Age." In other words, the Queen, the leader is laid to rest here. He believes that this refers again to the sleeping goddess, Ashtatara.

Let's step back a moment. At the time, our group of travelers knew nothing about translations of tablets from Burrows Cave. We knew only that sometime during our journey we were to awaken the Grail Codes, that there was a goddess from Atlantean times named Ashtatara (a name I couldn't even pronounce then), and that the Zeitlmairs and Francis Aloisio believed she was the sleeping goddess. So the following questions ran through our minds as we looked at the beguiling statue: "Did she have something to do with the dormant Grail Codes? Were we to awaken *her*? How would our mission to activate the Grail Codes unfold?"

Astonishingly, the awakening took place not in a prehistoric, windblown temple but in a hotel meeting room on the shores of St. Paul's Bay.

I had just finished channeling White Eagle for our group and many were getting anxious for dinner. But instead of coming back from my normal light trance, I went even further out. My head pitched back… something that had never happened before. Guttural sounds came from my mouth. I was embarrassed that I might actually be drooling, and I certainly dislike this sort of drama. Yet I was powerless to stop it. It felt like my consciousness was somewhere very deep, that I was climbing out of the dense earth itself. Even my arms moved as if to dig out of the depths. Part of me was frightened, because I had never experienced such a faraway state. In more than twenty years of channeling, I had only ever brought through White Eagle or Mark. I was uncertain what was happening here. The part of me that could still reason chose to surrender to what was happening; if I got into trouble, there were many gifted healers and energy workers in the group who could help put me back together again. I could hear people speaking to me, but I was too far away to respond. For a moment I thought this might be what it feels like to die: people are around you, but you can no longer reach them. In the spirit of an explorer, I let go.

After many minutes of effort, I spoke. Slowly, with pauses and sighs, I brought through the energy and the words of the goddess Ashtatara. All who were present could feel the immense presence and compassion that filled the room. It was electrifying and exquisite. Because of my struggle with her energy, her speech was stilted, yet she spoke loudly, with commanding authority:

*I am she who was called.
I speak with great difficulty
for the distances are too large
and the forgetting too deep.
I come because you called.
I come to bring you home.
I come to bring home here.
The world is nothing like you think.
You cannot think this world.
I have too much to say, but perhaps I speak better without words.
I carry with me a field of awakening that requires no words.
Everything you think you know about our people is wrong,
and it does not help you if you get it right.
This Earth is precious beyond measure.
The grail you seek cannot be understood,
but known only through your heart.
The Grail Codes are in you… asleep in you.
and you have called me to awaken them.
It has started.
The awakening of the codes has started.
You will not feel them.
You will not see them.
You cannot study them.
Only your heart knows them.
I have been protected by dragons for
over eighteen thousand years.
They are now released.
The gates to my world are open.
Stand with all your power and receive.
STAND with all your power!
I am she who has awakened.*

You are they who have awakened.
I dismiss you now.

Those in the room stood. Many felt cellular shifts. Some felt nothing at all. But all stood in silence in the knowing of the enormity of what had just transpired.

For the rest of our eight days on Malta our group visited temples, churches, and historic sites. We did ceremonies and meditations to activate the spirit of the wind. But nothing equaled the swift and silent transformation that we knew was the awakening of the Grail Codes… within us.

Ashtatara, Queen of Atlantis

Hubert and Dagmar Zeitlmair, through their translation of tablets removed from Burrows Cave and also from ten plates of ancient writing found on Malta, identified Ashtatara, the Mistress or Queen of Atlantis, as a highly developed being of celestial stock. Her husband was the pre-Flood master builder—known as the Lord Protector of Earth—Asuara Sidha. (Note: This is a proto-Sanskrit word, which differs slightly in spelling and meaning from the Sanskrit word "Siddha.") He was a godlike being of extraterrestrial origin, known in other cultures as Ra, Rama, and Poseidon. The Zeitlmairs' research led them to believe that Malta was this celestial couple's sacred headquarters. It is here the Lord Protector and his goddess left a legacy carved in stone: "They fused their stellar wisdom into the genetic makeup of their descendants, where it sleeps in the subconscious mind. The memory is dormant in some of us and needs only to be awakened.… To these humans the Spirits speak in a special way in the deepest part of their being. You may well be one of these individuals."[5]

The translation of the tablets says that 130,000 years ago the "Mighty Mother" gave birth to Asuara Sidha and Ashtatara. The Zeitlmairs believe that Asuara Sidha and Ashtatara were from an outlying planet of our solar system—Nibiru. Zecharia Sitchin was the first to write about the influence of beings from Nibiru, or planet X. He based this on his research into the myths and writings from ancient Babylonian and Sumerian civilizations. The theory of a celestial ancestry for our gods and even for the genetics of the human race is a common thread in ancient and native cultures. The oldest Egyptian lore claims a stellar connection for the gods Isis and Osiris—literally "of Sirius." The Dogon people of the Sahara claim connection to the dog stars of Sirius A and B. In the Americas the Hopi, the Cherokee, the Mayas, and other native tribes claim original descent from the Pleiades, as do some Aboriginals in Australia. Ancient temples and writings worldwide attest to profound technical knowledge of mathematics, astronomy, cosmology, and natural sciences that may have come originally from extraterrestrials, ages before the rise of major known civilizations.

The stone tablets describe the rise during the time of Atlantis of a materialistic, caste-dominated, imperialistic state in which people had forgotten their peaceful origins. Plato, in his dialogues on Atlantis, tells a similar story. Asuara Sidha, with his extraterrestrial ties, prepared to defend the Earth from the rise of power, greed, and rampant technology. His people dug deep into the ground, honeycombing whole mountains with tunnels and chambers to store supplies, equipment, and flying machines in the fight against the imperial state of Atlantis. They built underground passages for travel from one continent to another. A protracted war was fought. Asuara Sidha—the Lord and Protector of the Earth—was betrayed and killed, while his wife, Ashtatara the Queen of Atlantis, was put into a state of suspended animation, hidden and locked in a subterranean chamber. The chamber was sealed by a protective shield, or spiritual spell, until such time as she heeds the call from humanity to awaken.

The legends of ancient civilizations of advanced beings with incredible technology, constructing massive tunnels and storage chambers in the Earth, may seem farfetched, but stay with me, because these stories relate directly to what I discovered just six months later in a spiritual journey to Transylvania in Romania! Chapter 11 will talk more about these other mysteries.

All of what you have just read from the Zeitlmairs' research about Ashtatara—that she was put into a sleep under a protective shield, or spell, until she heeds the call from humanity—was unknown to me the evening in Malta when she first came through. In light of this, it is uncanny—even eerie—to recall that it felt like I was digging out from deep within the Earth and that her words through me echo the ancient legends:

> *I have been protected by dragons*
>   *for over eighteen thousand years.*
> *They are now released.*
> *The gates to my world are open.*

Of course, we are compelled to ask the question, "Was Ashtatara's spellbound burial place beneath the Mosta Dome?" The site of the current church certainly seemed to be spiritually protected. My spirit body couldn't pass through its dome in an earlier flying dream, a World War II bomb didn't explode when it hit the church, and Evalyn noticed dragons fleeing from the basement as we all prayed there. Hmm?

According to Hubert Zeitlmair, there is a Phoenician poem that describes a love story between Poseidon and his wife. The Phoenician version was a copy from earlier Egyptian hieroglyphics, which were no doubt from a far more ancient source. What I find particularly fascinating is that it matches the texts translated from the Burrows Cave stone tablets about the Queen of Atlantis being put into a state of suspension and protected under the earth by a spell:

> *He saw her hair as dark as charcoal. Beheld her beautiful ivory face with two big eyes that shone like diamonds, and orichalcum[1] lips that smelt of mace.*
>
> *From silky neck his gaze then wandered to golden breasts that looked aside; to waist and buttocks of white marble. That made his deep groin there abide.*
>
> *Poseidon loved her from that moment, adored her all; her proportions and her grace. Made her Queen of Atlantis, and Mistress of her race.*
>
> *Her bronzed body he made eternal, in his kingdom at his temple; to protect her he forced her within stone and everlasting spell.*
>
> *But SHE still lives amongst her people, Her kind and theirs did not immerse.*
>
> *Poseidon retained her body beneath deep rock and a curse.*

A Message on the Summer Solstice

I was anxious to spread the activation of the Grail Codes to others, who hadn't been with us in Malta. So, I organized a special event in Denver the next month for the summer solstice. My purpose was to once again call in Ashtatara. Forty people

---

[1] Wikipedia: "Orichalcum is a metal mentioned in several ancient writings, most notably the story of Atlantis as recounted in the Critias dialogue, recorded by Plato. According to Critias, orichalcum, considered second only to gold in value, was found and mined in many parts of Atlantis in ancient times."

sat in their chairs, waiting for the Atlantean goddess. Her power and strength were palpable as I brought through her words:

I AM THE AWAKENER!
Through the cold darkness
I have waited for the sun to come up once again
on my human brothers and sisters.
It is past time.
Each of you holds secrets locked and coded
within your consciousness and your body—
closed and locked for your own good.
When darkness befell humanity, much
of the power was removed,
the keys guarded closely.
The keys are where you never look; inside yourself.
My name is ASHTATARA.
It means "mother of the world."
I am a goddess and a human,
one of a race that remembers that
you are gods and goddesses too.
Once the doors begin to open,
the growth moves very quickly.
Once the doors are open there is no closing them.
ARE YOU READY?
The activation sequence is given in silence
at a level of consciousness that is barely awake in you.
I will move now into an initiation of silence.
I will speak again when it is done . . .
[Silence for about fifteen minutes]
. . . create the possibility of a much bigger you and
much more whole oneness . . .
Receive the love from this field in a way that

transforms everything you have been until now—
a love far beyond the emotional love;
a love that is the breath of God.

Receive now, deeply into your newly
awakened cells of light.
Be sanctified Beloved ones.
Be sanctified permanently now.
You now carry codes of awakening.
You do not need me anymore.
I leave you now.
DO NOT CALL ME BACK![2]

Once again we sat in silence, knowing that a profound change had taken place within us, and hopefully through us to the rest of humanity. I believe that as we incorporate spiritual changes the new knowledge becomes available to all humanity through our collective field. This can be likened to the hundredth-monkey effect.[3]

Can I admit that I was more than a little disappointed that Ashtatara had delivered such a stern warning at the end of her message about not calling her back again? The girl part of me had been looking forward to the rather glamorous possibility of channeling Ashtatara, the Queen of Atlantis, rather than just White Eagle and Mark. (Sorry guys.) But it was not to be. She was not a goddess to be disobeyed.

---

2 This was recorded and is for sale as a CD or audio download at www.JonetteCrowley.com.
3 The often-cited phenomenon whereby learned behavior spreads instantaneously throughout a population—monkeys in the original research—once a critical mass is reached.

The Solar Grail

As Ashtatara spoke, she showed me a symbol in my mind's eye. It seemed familiar, yet I was unsure where I'd seen it. An internet search revealed it to be an ancient Egyptian symbol: Originally the crown of the goddess Hathor, later it also became the crown of the goddess Isis and her son, the god Horus.

It was then that I realized she was showing me the hidden meaning behind the crown worn by the gods and goddesses of ancient times. The sphere represents the sun disc—our spirit or divine light, our soul. The surrounding vessel is our physical self—the grail—the vessel that holds our light. The chalice also signifies the feminine quality of wisdom. The disc is the masculine sun, the quality of will. The symbol is their merging—our own divine sun into our body. When body and soul are together, as they were meant to be, we are gods and goddesses too! As my spirit guide had so clearly stated, when he gave me the mission to activate the Grail Codes: "The Grail Codes are the other half of the Sun Disc Codes… together they form a new foundation for human consciousness."

Ashtatara said at her first appearance: "The Grail Codes are in you… asleep in you… The awakening of the codes has started." It was only after Ashtatara had come through a second time that I fully understood what the codes really were. I asked myself the question: "What is within every one of us that is coded?" The only answer: our DNA—the biological template of our physical existence. The activation that we'd received in silence was the awakening of our dormant DNA. It was as if an inner key, a primal code, was switched on.

Scientists have mapped the human genome to find that only about 3 percent of our DNA functions to instruct the cells. The purpose of the remaining 97 percent remains a mystery, initially even labeled as "junk" DNA. It is my belief that eons and eons ago, humans were highly developed, spiritual beings of light, utilizing 100 percent of our DNA. We were telepathic, clairvoyant, and wise; we could teleport; we didn't need to eat or struggle—in short, we lived as gods and goddesses upon the Earth. Then, as the ages passed, we lost our light and our abilities, our high vibrations diminished. You might say we fell from Paradise. We lost the use of the full power in our DNA. We atrophied. The 97 percent of our DNA fell into disuse.

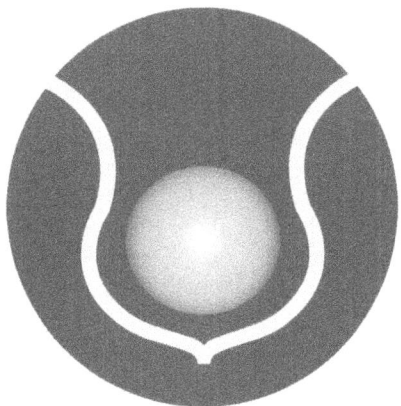

The crown of Isis. Fig. 3.3

As much as we try to grow spiritually, we have been stopped because our biology, our physical vessel, can't support the higher frequencies of light for which we yearn. Reactivating our DNA, our dormant codes, creates once again the physical vessel—the grail—that can hold our highest spirit. Awakening isn't merely about experiencing high levels of spiritual light, but also containing and integrating it into our physiology and material world. The Egyptians and early mystery schools understood the significance of the grail and sun disc combined; after all, the symbol of integration of spirit and matter, light and form, solar disc and vessel was *the* crown delineating a god or goddess! When the sun disc energies and the Grail Codes are awakened, *we* are the new gods of light! So this activation was a huge event for us all!

The grail was never just the cup of Jesus from the Last Supper, or even the bloodline of Jesus through Mary Magdalene. **We are the Holy Grail!** What is happening now is the merging of our divinity into our humanity. The Grail Codes are our unused DNA! Through the words and energies of a long-sleeping goddess, our very DNA was awakened in a way that a few months later would lead to my discovery of a simple process for bringing our soul's light into our cells—Soul Body Fusion. I use this symbol, which I now call the "Solar Grail," as the symbol for Soul Body Fusion.

Isis, fig. 3.4

Please take a few minutes to slowly reread the previous passages from Ashtatara. Allow the words to sink into your cells, enhancing your magnificence. Savor the energies. These phrases begin the Soul Body Fusion process by activating your DNA to hold more of your light. For some, Ashtatara's energy field and her words break open a floodgate of feelings, sensations, and changes. However, I promise that you don't need to feel anything to have a profound shift occur. Once the activation is given, it spreads throughout the human matrix, empowering each of us to become beings of light—Christed humans. Ashtatara's job is done. She waited eighteen thousand years for the time when humans would be guided to her and ready to receive her secret. Now it belongs to us—each of us.

Let's get back to Ashtatara, also known as the Mother Goddess. Because she was the goddess (or queen) of Atlantis—before the great Flood—we might speculate that she was the original goddess, and that many of the post-Flood goddesses sprang from her legends. If this is correct, she would be the predecessor of Ashtaroth, Ishtar, Asherah, Inanna, Ashtarte, Astarte, Ishara, Istar, Istaru, Aschtar, Aschtart, Tara, Ashtottara, Hathor, Isis, Aphrodite, and Venus. Understanding this, it comes as no surprise that she is connected to the symbol that crowns Hathor and Isis.

More Magic in the Symbol

Let's move forward in time to illustrate the power and perhaps hidden spiritual meaning of the sun disc and grail symbol that Ashtatara showed me.

For the December solstice of 2010, I was guided to take a group to Egypt to do special ceremonies in the Great Pyramid and between the paws of the Sphinx. (Please see more details in Chapter 12).

Everywhere in Egypt we saw the symbol crowning Hathor, Isis, and Horus. However, there is a special column at the Hathor Temple in Queen Hatshepsut's immense complex near Luxor where the crown isn't perched on the head of a god or goddess. It is pictured alone, but—more remarkably—upside down. One of its hornlike sides merges into a cobra, a symbol of awakened kundalini energy.[4] The cobra's body passes through an ankh, the Egyptian key of life. Anne from Denmark had an extraordinary experience there.

Column at Hatshepsut's Temple, Egypt.
(Fig. 3.5 Photo by Anne Risager)

> *As I walked up the temple stairs I felt the energies pushing me into another dimension. I felt I was wearing the mask of Anubis: the jackal-headed god who is the gatekeeper. Since our tour guide Hassan had talked about the columns of Hathor being like sistrums [ancient protective percussion instruments], I selected a pillar and approached it, asking permission to shake "the sistrum." At that moment a very deep sound rang in my inner*

---

4 "Kundalini" means "coiled" in Sanskrit. It refers to powerful life force energy coiled in the sacrum that moves up the spine when awakened. It is sometimes called the sleeping serpent.

ear, vibrating, pushing atoms aside as if the sound was clearing its way. I felt the skies pull apart, drawing aside curtains of stars, revealing layer upon layer to an inner dimension of the cosmos.

Then stellar energies started pouring down. It felt like a blessing—a shower of stars flooding my body. As the energies built, I felt the cobra rising through my spine, settling in my forehead.[5] I find it so fascinating is that the hieroglyphs on the pillar directly explained what I experienced! Hassan later told me that the inverted crown of Isis represents stellar energies pouring down.

This hints at a deeper meaning for the symbol. It pours stellar energies into us, awakening our central energies, or kundalini—bringing enlightenment—for those who know how to ask for it.

Completing the Activation of the Four Elements

During our time in Malta, we completed the activation of the last of the four physical elements—air. What started in Nepal to activate earth, then to Peru to activate water, and to Mount Kilimanjaro to activate fire, would finish here in the Mediterranean. We chose to do it on the small island of Gozo, at Ggantija, site of two megalithic temples—some of the oldest free-standing stone monuments known to humankind. In perfect timing, the wind blew with the force and determination of a gale. In a meditation we opened our hearts so much that we felt one with Mother Earth. We felt her water as our blood, her earth as our

---

5 In Egypt, the cobra, or uraeus, on the forehead is the mark of a deity, or pharaoh.

flesh, her fire as our energy. We felt the air that ignited our spirit as we breathed it in and out. It is the air more than anything else that connects us to the Mother.

The completion of these four Earth-activation journeys created a space in us and in the Earth that awakened in a new way the four ancient elements that comprise physical matter. The four form a container—a grail—for the arrival of the fifth and most important element: spirit (sometimes called ether.) When the physical is prepared, the spirit moves in. As you activate your lost DNA codes, as you integrate and fully occupy your beloved body, you are ready for the presence of spirit to enter your life and your world in a way never before possible.

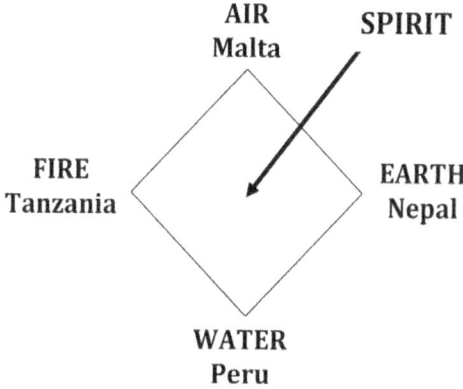

The activation of the five elements. Fig. 3.6

Let's now learn Soul Body Fusion, a radically simple tool that helps you embody your spirit for a whole you.

PART II

The Process

You are learning a skill that is your birthright. From you it moves out into the human matrix, repairs broken meridians, and reestablishes the electrical system that enables soul, light, spirit, and enlightenment to move into humankind. The process is not linear, which makes it both easy and hard to learn. It is easy to do.

—Mark

Chapter 4

The Birth of the Soul Body Fusion Process

People keep struggling with problems both physical and mental, never suspecting the root cause: that the bond between body and soul has been severed... It takes effort to keep your soul at a distance. When you stop struggling, the path to the soul is automatic.
  -Dr. Deepak Chopra

Here Is How It Started

In September, 2007, just four months after our awakening in Malta, I was in New Mexico, speaking at a conference titled "The Quantum Leap." Early one morning, I was reading a book by Michael Newton, PhD, *Destiny of Souls*. Newton used hypnotic regression with his clients to explore past lives and the activities of the soul in between incarnations.

The passage that caught my attention was a transcript from a female client under regression. She explained her experience of when a soul joins a human body: "When souls enter the human body on Earth they come into dense matter. Their host bodies, after all, contain primitive animal energy which is thick. The soul has a natural sort of pure, refined energy which does not easily blend with some human hosts. It takes some experience to get used to all this."[6]

Newton describes the soul as intelligent light energy that "appears to function as vibrational waves similar to electromagnetic force." He states: "Body energy and soul energy are adversely affected by vibrational resonances not in harmony with each other. Each person has his/her own fingerprint of natural rhythms. Body and soul must smoothly coexist for humans to be productive."[7]

Now I was concerned. The very thought that our body and soul could adversely affect each other, was a totally new idea to me. How could that be? I had always assumed that soul and body fit together like hand and glove. "Hmm," I thought, "I wonder if *mine* are in harmony. This might explain a lot."

So, sitting on my hotel room bed, I closed my eyes and asked my mind to locate the frequency of my body. When I had the subtle knowing that I was connected to it, I asked to locate the frequency of my soul. Then I compared the two vibrations. I noticed that although they weren't actually fighting each other, they certainly didn't coexist in supportive harmony. This situation wasn't going to get me the enlightened life I envisioned. Wondering if I could somehow fix it, I reasoned that if I got to a high enough frequency there must be a place where the energy fields of both my body and soul would automatically merge. So I imagined grabbing the vibrational field of my body by one hand, my soul by the other, and punching "up" in an imaginary, spiritual elevator; stopping when the separation between the two was healed and they were both dancing to a new, higher vibrational melody. Then I figured I needed a way to make the merging permanent, so I silently declared that this place would be my new base of being. In a sense I "book marked" the state. I meditated ten minutes more, holding as precisely as I could to this space of harmony within me.

At no time did I feel anything or see anything. I did it all by intention, imagination, and assumption. Since I wasn't sure whether anything had really changed, I said out loud to the universe, "I want CLEAR confirmation if what I did worked." Then I went to breakfast at the hotel restaurant.

I sat with people I hadn't met before. The conversation provided ringing confirmation that a change had happened and it was visible to others. The first comment was immediate: "You look so radiant this morning." Can you imagine? This was *before* breakfast!

Then another woman said something that indicated I'd needed the shift: "Jonette, we loved your talk yesterday, but sometimes your vibration didn't always connect with the audience. But several times your energy *did* come down to a place where we could all get what you were projecting. Then you really connected."

What I heard was that when I come from my soul place but am not integrated into my body, I am not connecting to others. "Can this be one of the reasons I haven't reached as many people as I would have liked?" I thought to my self.

Over our meal one woman admitted, "I have a shield up that keeps me from attracting more clients, and there is sadness in me. I don't know where it's from." I offered to do this new energy process with her. Here I go. Having discovered this tool only an hour earlier, I'm already trying it out with others. It is this approach of experimenting and testing that has taught me what I'm sharing in this book.

As we sat at the conference, I touched her back and imagined holding her in a high space, asking that her blocks dissolve and that her spirit and body move into harmony with each other. As a sensitive person, she could feel the blending take place, again providing confirmation that something significant occurred at a physical level. The next day she was the radiant one, telling me that the block to abundance seemed to have moved, because people were seeking her out to work with them.

I was excited that something happened with no effort! So I recruited several people at the conference with whom to experiment. At this point I had no name for the process. The first person was Ewa (pronounced "Eva"), a Polish medical doctor living in England, who admitted that she could help everyone but herself. Her current practice had taken her beyond the medical model to spiritual and energy healing. She came to me for a White Eagle reading, after which I offered to do this brand-new energy work with her. During our session I didn't touch her. I simply sat quietly, holding the intention that her soul and body would align. Embarrassed, she burped often and loudly, a great sign that deep physical integration was taking place. After a few minutes, the emerging flow seemed to hit a block in her solar plexus. We did nothing but wait, trusting in the intelligence of the process.

Moments later, Ewa burst into deep sobs of grief. She described it as sadness in being separated from herself for so long. She told me that her hands finally felt reconnected to her. She stroked the skin on her arms, exclaiming, "I have never felt my body before." Heat and tingling were running through her as if she were plugged into an electrical outlet. To me it felt like her new brightness had changed her cells. They seemed to move into a plasma dimension—not fluid but no longer solid—where they resonated in accordance with her soul's energy. The healing was so deep it was as if she had experienced psychic surgery. She returned to her hotel room to sleep the rest of the day.

Here are Ewa's words to me as she recalled that autumn day in 2007:

> I was already in the experience, walking the lawn and the few steps to your hotel room. From there, we went deep into the most exquisite feelings! I cried, as I often do when I feel the LOVE of the Spirit, and on this occasion especially as the great presence of ALL involved was celebrating ME! I continued weeping softly till the very end, like a child overwhelmed and moved to tears. It was so good… so good and so sweet! I could have sat there forever, feeling this embrace. That feeling stayed with me a long time.
>
> Now, as for the Soul Body Fusion, from my professional work I would say that every soul-healing incident is a soul body fusion experience. Most of these are small steps and may even be unconscious, especially at the beginning of the awakening journey. I have witnessed in my own practice that the intention of the client and the facilitator can speed up the process, allowing for major leaps. With all the help available currently and with our own increased awareness, we can facilitate the integration of the soul to a degree unthinkable not so long ago! This is only possible with the expansion of consciousness that we are all co-creating.

Three years after my very first Fusion experience with Ewa, I met Micela, who was Ewa's roommate at the conference in New Mexico. Here are Micela's words describing the shift she observed in her good friend Ewa after our session:

> Ewa told me she was to have a session with you [Jonette]. I went out and didn't come back until af-

ter dinner. Upon my return, the closer I came to our place, the more I felt an unfamiliar sensation all over my body. I remember this moment vividly: laughingly I said out loud, "Gosh, this feels like walking against a strong wind, as if inside the bungalow a huge tornado is still in action." There was a strong energy wrapped around the entire place. The moment I entered the room, something profound ran throughout my body. A part of me was clearly aware that I was witness to something beyond everything I had ever experienced so far, something beyond words.

Ewa was sleeping. However, all I could feel was a huge shift in progress. An immense power was emanating from her side of the room, which seemed to reach out to me as I collapsed into my bed. I remember flashes of images as if her body was caught up in a spiraling transformative response. The next morning Ewa was so joyful. I must say, normally Ewa is not so "spot on" in the morning. Something quite profound had changed.

It was a monumental experience for me personally. From that day on, there was a natural warmth, peace, gentleness, and divinity within and around Ewa. She was filled with light and life. It was as if something had lifted her burden. Anais Nin wrote, "There are very few human beings who receive the truth, complete and staggering, by instant illumination. Most of them acquire it fragment by fragment… by successive developments, cellularly, like a… mosaic." Today I can say Ewa was one of those who received the truth by instant illumination!

At the time, Micela had no idea that Ewa had experienced what I would later call a Soul Body Fusion. "Now it all makes sense," Micela admitted when I told her three years later. After my experience with Ewa and several others on that first day, I began to consider the implications of bringing our soul into alignment with our physical body. We can be more present and grounded in our life and therefore increasingly magnetic to the things we want. After all, how can we attract what we want when we're not fully home? Having a higher vibration in our body can magnetize health and well-being, while repelling negativity and dis-ease. It can be easier to be in the flow, more abundant, happier, have greater influence… the possibilities are endless. I guess the conference really was a "Quantum Leap" for me.

Within a week, my spirit guide Mark gave me the name—Soul Body Fusion®. (It is now a registered trademark, taking the symbol®.) Soul is first because the soul is in charge of the process.

Following my initial success, I asked White Eagle, "Can I teach others to do this too?" His reply was uncharacteristically open-ended: "I don't know. Try it."

Two months later we had a pilot class to teach people to do Soul Body Fusions on themselves and others. It was a resounding success. Those early students have continued to develop the process, always adding to our body of knowledge as we go along.

Now I understand that White Eagle's answer offered greater guidance than I first perceived. "Try it" has been the main mantra for Soul Body Fusion.

How Do We Fuse in the First Place?

From his regression work Michael Newton states: "Souls join their assigned hosts in the womb of the baby's mother sometime after the third month of pregnancy so they will have a sufficiently evolved brain to work with before term. As part of the fetal state they are still able to think as immortal souls while they get used to brain circuitry and the alter ego of their host."[8]

Machaelle Small Wright, a spiritual pioneer with the ability to see and hear the invisible forces in nature, has been an inspiration to many through her books. From her communications with the intelligence of nature and the devic kingdom, she has created flower essences and an understanding of how and why they can be used. I discovered her downloadable article *Body/Soul Fusion Process: A Flower Essence Process for Newborns, Infants, Older Children, & Adults*. Machaelle Small Wright's detailed explanations of the body/soul connection were intriguing and felt intuitively right to me.

She wrote that in order for the soul to experience life on Earth, it must combine with form/nature to create a single functioning unit. In other words, the soul is seeking to experience life by combining with physical reality. She learned in her communications with the wisdom of nature—which is the power of all physical form—that there are three stages of bonding between soul and body:

1. **A magnetic-like link.** The first connection is at conception, when the soul force makes a magnetic-like link with the fertilized egg. The linkage is based on the principle of like attracting like. As the link strengthens, the fetus and soul accommodate each other. Small Wright indicates that "if the form is unable to develop in ways that are appropriate to and necessary for the soul's purpose and function, the soul will initiate a disconnection and the magnetic-like link will cease." The mother will experience a miscarriage. "A miscarriage will not occur with an inspirited fetal form."

2. **Electrical connection.** The next level of connection occurs electrically at around the seventh month of preg-

nancy. Prior to this the fetal electrical system is insufficiently developed to support the fusion. Small Wright states: "The fusion mechanism is centered in the electrical system, primarily. It then directly impacts the molecular system."

3. **Molecular fusion.** The final molecular fusion may occur anytime after the seventh month of gestation. Machaelle Small Wright believes that by birth the baby's electrical and cellular systems have fully received the soul. However, some souls don't fuse until the time of birth, and some take several months to two years to fully fuse.

From a global perspective, I see that humanity as a whole and each of us as individuals have divine blueprints that exist magnetically in the cosmos. The bridges that connect the divine template to our physical world seem to be electrical in nature. Over eons, either through humanity's own poor choices or from outside influences, these electrical bridges have become broken down, disabling the smooth flow of wisdom and light from the universe into our physical world. More than anything else, Soul Body Fusion seems to repair the electrical connections between our physical form and our divine heritage. That is one reason why many people experience the Fusion so electrically. As more people integrate their highest light physically we are strengthening the template of harmony and oneness between the entire spiritual and physical realms. Richard Gerber, MD, author of *Vibrational Medicine*, describes matter and energy as primarily electrical.

Interestingly, etheric and astral frequencies that are beyond the speed of light are primarily magnetic. The physical universe exhibits the law of entropy, where order tends to move to chaos. On the other hand, the world of the soul, beyond time and space, exhibits negative entropy—where chaos moves to order and organization—thus enabling regeneration and healing.⁹ In this context, with Soul Body Fusion we are merging the higher world of infinite order and wholeness into our relatively chaotic physical realm.

How Did We Become Unfused?

Again, no one who is alive is totally unfused. However, all of us walk around in varying levels of alignment between our spirit and our form. Here are some answers I get when I ask participants in workshops, "What are some reasons that the soul might not be completely integrated?"

- Birth trauma
- Abuse
- Lack of interest in being born in the first place
- Sense of not being wanted
- Sickness
- Physical pain
- Abandonment
- Fear
- Chronic stress
- Shock
- Negative judgment about our body
- Strong ego attachment
- Religion—we are sinners/unclean
- Guilt
- Loss, grief, disappointment

- Unsafe surroundings
- Emotional/mental disorders
- Alcoholism/addictions
- Over-sensitivity
- Lack of self-love
- Feeling of not being good enough

Another reason a soul may not be completely embodied is that we have been constantly reminded just how unworthy our body is. Growing up in the Catholic Church, I remember there was a point in the Mass, before we received Communion, in which we knelt down in prayer, thumped our heart, and repeated three times: "I am not worthy to receive you… " Imagine the impact on human consciousness from millions of Catholics, billions of Masses, down the centuries—pounding repeatedly into their hearts "I am not worthy."

I'm sorry to say that in our Christian religions the programming of our innate lack of perfection begins as children. As a six-year-old, I remember being asked in Sunday school to draw a picture of my soul. With a sharpened number-two pencil in hand, I conscientiously sketched my smiling face, my skinny arms and legs, and my torso— with a rather pillow shaped soul inside it. Then taking the edge of my pencil, I filled the space inside my soul with dirty lead smudges—my sins, because we all knew that everyone is a sinner, even a six-year-old. In the same vein, I was told of a woman who was concerned about merging with her soul during her Fusion because she considered her soul as a vessel for sins!

One of the most dramatic examples I have ever seen of an unfused soul and body was my work with a highly spiritual woman who was ready to commit suicide. She wasn't angry or depressed. She was simply done. I channeled White Eagle for her in the midst of her crisis. He explained that she had a beautiful soul, but it existed almost completely above her head, with little or no connection to her body. I observed as White Eagle helped her slowly bring her powerful light down into her body, healing the lifelong separation. It turns out that she had been sexually abused since she was a toddler. There was so much pain in her body that her full soul couldn't come in. This caused her to want to die. Today she is a gifted and important spiritual teacher.

My Body Is Divine

Years ago I taught a series of courses called "Healer/Healer." The premise was that it is in partnership that we heal—ourselves and each other. It's not about one person being a healer and the other needing to be fixed. My guides suggested we begin the workshop with what seemed to be a simple exercise in pairs. Person A stayed on the chair, while his/her partner B sat on the floor in front, touching the top of A's feet. Then from the floor, B would look into the other's eyes, repeating "Your body is Divine" for three or four minutes, emphasizing the four words differently, as came naturally.

"How hard can that be?" I thought as my partner repeated the mantra, "Your body is Divine," while grounding the truth of it into me by touching my feet. Within fifteen seconds, I had tears glistening in my eyes. After a minute, a dam of resistance broke through; tears poured down my face as I fully and deeply accepted the words.

We are asked to accept our full body divinity now—not when we're perfect by some arbitrary standards. My strong reaction came as a shock because I *thought* that I liked and accepted my body.

Try It Yourself

Please find a way to do this simple exercise with a friend or partner. At the very least, imagine someone telling you firmly and repeatedly, "Your body is Divine." Stay with it, especially if it is emotionally uncomfortable. Our body must be willing to accept its divinity. After all, our soul is just our personal piece of the Divine.

How far apart are *your* soul and body? Test it yourself. For a moment, please close your eyes and ask to sense the vibration of your body. Once you think you have it—trust your instincts here, as it probably won't feel concrete— ask to find the vibration of your soul. On a scale of 1 to 10 (with 1 being closely harmonized and 10 being miles apart), how closely aligned is your spirit and form? If there is room for improvement—keep reading.

Chapter 5

Fusing Your Soul

Soul Body Fusion is such a simple tool, but at the same time—the core of the whole truth. It is a way to become who we really are—and nothing is more important than this.

-Thomas, Denmark

Your Soul Is in Charge

For the sake of simple understanding, let's say that your mind is made up of two aspects. One is your ego, or personality-centered self. It operates in a mostly linear, logical way in the three-dimensional world—governed by your human will, emotions, belief systems, and the desire to protect you. It gets most of its information through your five senses and therefore resonates in step with the surrounding mass consciousness.

The higher part of your mind transcends your everyday limitations. It is awareness, or consciousness itself. It exists in the dimensions of love and truth and knows the world in a holistic way. We'll define soul as that part of universal consciousness that has a unique and specific identity like a fingerprint. Each person's soul has its own frequency, pattern, and vibrational signature that are recognizable in the higher worlds.

People often ask, "What is the difference between soul and spirit?" For our discussion, we'll say that soul is the assumed personal subset of spirit. They are both comprised of the same "stuff," the same quantum capabilities. Soul is that part of spirit that we recognize as our own. Soul grows as our recognition of these higher fields of consciousness expands. Ultimately we should be able to extend the boundaries of our awareness into the infinite reaches of spirit. We move from a small sense of "me," to a sense of "we," to the experience of "all-that-is."

The soul is not a limited entity with defined boundaries. You can't integrate it once and be done with it, because the soul itself, and its relationship to the body are dynamic. The soul's world is the infinitely sourced and interconnected—holographic universe. Think of your soul as an ever-expanding instrument of awareness that enables you to experience the multidimensional nature of the universe. We create from the level of our primary awareness. As your awareness increases, so does the recognition of your connection to the all-that-is. Although for the sake of language we'll speak as if the soul were a "thing," you might consider it a doorway to a complex, intelligent space. Your soul's intelligence, impulses and guidance manifest in the highest good for you and the world.

The beauty and simplicity of the Soul Body Fusion process stems from the fact that your soul is in charge. Everything that happens is under the loving direction of your spirit. Once your personality-centered self issues the invitation for alignment, your soul takes over. The small you isn't directing the outcome, so it can't block the process or do anything wrong. No matter what happens in the process, including having experiences that aren't comfortable—such as sadness, tiredness, pain—it is all for your greatest good under the wise direction of your soul. Period.

It's Your Birthright

You are God on Earth, divinity in form. You have infinite potential for a miraculous life. For so long we have forgotten how to be divine that now we doubt if it's even possible. Although most of us have a deep yearning for our greater potential, our habit, and history keep us small. Soul Body Fusion is a tool to reclaim who we've always been.

Knowing ourselves as whole, united beings of light in form is our destiny, and thus Soul Body Fusion is easy. There are three basic reasons why it works:

1. It's natural
2. It uses the magic of intention
3. It is based on the principle of resonance

It's Natural. Your spirit *wants* to be in form on Earth. That is why you were born here. It actually takes more energy to stay separate. For most people the physical sensations are immediate during a Fusion process, as if a dam of separation has been broken and your soul's energy comes rushing in.

The Magic of Intention. Your focused thought is the most powerful tool on the planet. Intention creates the connection. Intention finds your body's frequency. Intention locates the frequency of your soul. Intention lifts them both to a harmonized pattern. Intention directs the complex biological shifts in your cells.

Your imagination is intention's greatest ally. Create the pictures you want in your mind. Play. It can be as easy as P.I.E. **Pretend. Imagine. Experiment!**

Intention is the act of conscious choice. Without clear intention there is no focus. No focus means that you will passively resonate to mass consciousness that surrounds you. Remember: thought creates. In fact, it is the only thing that does.

The Principle of Resonance. Your physical body has a unique vibrational pattern that creates an energetic field of resonance. The same is true for your soul. Before Fusion the two fields may not be in harmony. For some people, who are greatly disassociated, it may feel as if their body and soul are actually in conflict. On the other end of the spectrum are people who already enjoy a great deal of integration between their spiritual and physical selves. In either case, more merging can always occur.

The downward-pointing triangle represents soul. The upward pointing triangle is the body. At times they feel disconnected or misaligned. Soul Body Fusion brings them together. Fig.5.1

Your intention to harmonize your physicality with your spirit strengthens the link. Once the connection is established, the vibrations of each begin to merge, creating a new, blended harmonic. Scientifically speaking, there is an entrainment of diverse vibrational patterns. Gregg Braden, best-selling author, describes entrainment as an "alignment of forces, or flows of energy, to allow maximum transfer of information or communication." In practice, the slower vibratory rate of the body synchronizes to the faster rate of the soul. Again, this supports our spiritual law that consciousness always moves to a higher platform.

There is yet another way in which resonance plays a part in the Fusion process. When you do a Fusion, your intention connects you to the resonant field of all the people who already operate at a high level of spiritual harmony. Just by reading this book, you are resonating to a higher field. Can you feel changes in your body already? If you receive a Fusion by watching me demonstrate on a video or in front of an audience, or even listen on the radio, you are connecting to a field that carries a fused soul and body. Once you've received a Fusion and then do it on others, your newly fused resonant field entrains with theirs, making the process more powerful for them.

To summarize, Soul Body Fusion as a process is so uncomplicated because your intention connects the energy fields of your soul and body, then resonance attunes them into higher harmony—all because it is your natural state of being!

No Rules

Soul Body Fusion is a simple process of spiritual realignment that you can learn from a trained facilitator, by watching a video, by taking a class, or by reading this book. Our website (www.SoulBodyFusion.com) has articles, videos, links and resources, including a directory of Certified Teachers. After reading this book, feel free to do Fusions on family and friends. However, if you wish to have a greater understanding and practice, we suggest you enroll in a one or two-day course taught by Certified Teachers around the world. This is especially helpful if you want to confidently do Soul Body Fusions on others—even make this the basis of a professional healing or energy work practice. In this chapter, I'll walk you through the process and what you might expect. In the next chapter, you will learn how to do a Fusion on another. Chapter 7 has more information on healing and healers.

The reason I am giving you everything you need to know to do Soul Body Fusions on yourself and others is that the world is changing rapidly and we must have all of our powers available as fast as possible, both individually and collectively. Soul Body Fusion is simple and powerful and belongs to everyone. My personal mission is to explore new processes and hidden wisdom; then to solidify the knowledge so the processes are clear and replicable. Finally, to share it everywhere, as fast as I can! I believe that some people and organizations in the past held onto knowledge to gain importance, power, or wealth. That time is over.

My intention is for enough of us to wholly integrate the higher dimensions of our being into the physical, that this leverages humanity through a spontaneous quantum leap into a field of consciousness that supports harmony with the Earth, peace, health, and abundance. Are you in?

The Soul Body Fusion process has evolved through practice and experimentation. In the beginning I spent considerable time doing Fusions on clients, sometimes touching their hands, sometimes not. It works the same either way. Then I noticed that if I have a lot of time, it will take a lot of time. If I have only a few minutes, that is all it takes to get the process started. Several years ago I was speaking at a mind, body, spirit expo in Helsinki, Finland. During the weekend scores of people crowded around my table, asking whether I could do Soul Body Fusions on them. Until that moment I had taken at least forty-five minutes per person. Given the large number of people waiting and the limited time, I made a leap-of faith decision: I would do Fusions in ten minutes each! We pulled two chairs together at the side of the noisy cafeteria. My friend Tuija organized the waiting list—and I was in business! In just ten minutes most people experienced energetic shifts and physical sensations. My job was just to get the process rolling.

Later, I wondered whether I could do Fusions remotely over the telephone, since I've been doing channeled readings that way for years. I tried it and found that geographical distance made no difference. Then I pondered if I could do Soul Body Fusions via video clip. I tried it. From the emails I received once the video was posted, it was clear that this was also effective. It worked even when I was separated from the recipient in both space and time. Could it work through an audio transmission on an internet radio program? Sure enough, the responses poured in, confirming that the power of this little process is not dependent on the delivery method at all. I did Soul Body Fusion from the stage at a conference. Again, people reported amazing and often instantaneous changes. This is proof to me that we aren't *doing* anything in the traditional sense. Somehow, by the power of intention and the magic of expanding consciousness, it all simply happens.

First, let me clarify the limitations of language in describing this process. Although I use the words "do" and "give" Soul Body Fusion, in reality the only thing you "do" is set the intention for the soul and body to align. In another instance, I may say "bring in your soul." Of course, your soul and body are already connected. This phrase indicates that we are aligning our cells to even higher aspects of our spirit.

Remember that Soul Body Fusion works so easily because, one, it is natural; two, it uses the power of intention; and three, it works through resonance. For these reasons, it is irrationally simple. The biggest issue in learning Soul Body Fusion is wanting to make it more complex and add too many limitations and rules. Almost every time I've gone beyond my own guidelines, the process still works! In fact, Soul Body Fusion is so simple it can hardly be called a process. I often say there are "No Rules." Just try it. Thomas A. Edison said it best: "Hell, there are no rules here—we're trying to accomplish something."

Guidelines

What follows are general guidelines for doing Soul Body Fusion on yourself.

1. Set your intention.
State out loud or silently that it is your intention for the frequencies of your body to align with the frequencies of your soul or spirit. You intend that your cells adapt to permanently hold more of your own light, energy, divinity, god-self, higher self… whatever words are most comfortable. This is the step that invokes your soul. Please don't worry about how the intention is stated. Most of the time the intention is already clear because of your actions. You are reading this book, aren't you? I often find that the process has begun working even before these steps are followed. Did you feel shifts when you bought the book? When you read the words from Ashtatara? You see, the power is so strong that it can't actually be contained in a process.

2. Sit with your feet on the floor and your palms facing up.
The reason your feet are on the floor is to assist you in feeling grounded. Can you receive it lying down? Sure, if that feels right to you. Remember: No Rules. These are helpful guidelines. Your palms are facing upward because in many instances people feel

energy, warmth, laser lights coming into their palms. This position facilitates the experience.

3. Be present. Stay in your body. Don't meditate.
This is important because the objective is to integrate your higher dimensions into your body and into your everyday life, not to continue the separation of spirit and matter. Often, it may be your habit to leave your body and move into a meditative state as soon as higher frequencies of spirit are experienced. That is not the point! Stay grounded, present, and solidly in your body.

4. Observe your experience.
   Don't judge, analyze, compare, or fix.
The easiest way to remain centered is to give yourself the job of observing what happens during the process. Are your hands getting warm? Do you feel tingling? What is happening in your legs and feet? Your arms? What else is changing? What do you *feel,* physically and emotionally? I emphasize feeling so you won't be thinking too much. Simply note what you are experiencing and be open to insights. Don't try to figure out why and don't try to change it, push it, or fix it. Trust the process. If your right leg feels something and your left leg doesn't—fine. Your experience is exactly what it should be. Every sensation, whether pleasant or not, is perfect. If you feel nothing at all—perfect. No judgment. The most difficult part of this simple process is: Don't *do* anything.

During the Fusion you might want to visualize finding the frequency or feeling of your soul and connecting it to the frequency of your body. Be open to whatever happens. You may get clarity on old issues or clearing of the past, which can lead to tremendous healing.

Do Soul Body Fusion on Yourself

For the first time, allow yourself about twenty-five minutes. You might want to get paper and a pen to write down what you experience. Also, take a moment to get a glass of water. Drinking water will assist your body to integrate the influx of energy. During the process, stay very present—not meditating. Miscellaneous sounds in your environment shouldn't affect you. Over the years I have developed a simple protocol that works whether I am doing a Fusion on myself, with another person, or intending that the whole world receives it remotely.

Phase One: Ten Minutes
Please reread the above guidelines. Give your personality the job of witnessing all the details of what is happening to you physically. This keeps your mind from wandering. Set the intention for your soul and body to merge more completely, sit with your palms face up, and observe what you feel in your body for approximately ten minutes. I find that ten minutes is usually enough time for most people to feel shifts and sensations.

Take a Break
After ten minutes of sitting and observing, take a few moments to break the flow and to integrate. You may want to jot down what you experienced. This practical task of writing keeps you grounded and gives you a record to revisit. Remind yourself that your soul or higher self is in charge. Whether it is an enlightening experience, an uncomfortable one, or if nothing changes: it is all perfect. Drink water. Staying hydrated for the next few days is important. As your cells expand to accept the higher frequencies of your soul, toxins and cellular trash are sometimes released. Plenty of water helps wash the refuse away and keeps you from getting what I call a "detox" headache.

Phase Two: Ten Minutes
Now you are ready to repeat the Fusion for another ten minutes. Because of the energetic break, we often see that the next ten-minute phase is a very different experience. Doing two phases, even if you only have time for five minutes per phase, is better than a Fusion without the short break. I did remote Soul Body Fusions over the phone for the entire executive team of a high-tech company. Because of time constraints I only had a total of ten minutes per person. One gentleman, a brilliant mathematician and inventor, told me after the first five-minute phase: "I felt nothing. I never feel anything… just resistance… like there is a big wall round me."

"Fine," I responded. "Keep your palms up and we'll do the same thing for another five minutes." It is important that we make no judgments about the experience.

After the second phase everything had shifted for him: "I felt a big change. I'm in a place of peace like I've never felt before. Wow. This is *really* something. I hope I can keep this."

Concluding the Fusion
Drink more water and write down your impressions. What did you observe in your body? It is helpful to simply note what you *experienced*, not what you *think* about it. Check in with your intuition. Do you need to do the Fusion process a third time? Do you need to go to bed? Do you want fresh air? Do you need to move? to dance? Some people feel as if they have just had surgery and they go to bed for twelve to fourteen hours straight. Others feel so energized that they clean out every closet in the house. Most often you will want to spend time alone in order to integrate. Ask yourself, "What is the most supportive action for me right now?" Follow your intuition.

Now, before you read any further and get too many expectations in your head, do a Fusion on yourself.

What to Expect

What you might experience during the Soul Body Fusion runs the gamut from absolutely nothing to explosive kundalini awakening. No two people are the same.

- Energy, waves
- Tingling, bubbling, fizzing
- Heat and warmth
- Well-being, joy, bliss, peace
- Pressure in the heart or rapid heart beating
- Ringing in the ears
- Various pains
- Third Eye opening or pulsing
- Movement and changes in the brain
- Cells coming alive or popping like popcorn
- Pressure around the head
- Grief, sadness, crying
- Electric currents
- Vibrating, shaking, buzzing
- Euphoria
- Laughing, dancing
- Swaying, moving
- Burping, itching, tickling
- Giddy, silly, light-headed
- Grounded, solid, present
- Feeling my body in a totally new way
- Sick, nauseated, uncomfortable

- Quiet, still, silent
- Feeling like I'm coming home
- Heavy, dense
- Free, light, open, weightless

The most common feeling is that your cells are literally vibrating, tingling, and opening up. In Norway, some practitioners call Soul Body Fusion "Champagne Healing" because it feels as if your body is full of tiny, sparkling golden champagne bubbles! The changes often feel electrical. It is like you are being totally rewired to hold a much, much stronger current of higher frequencies and energies in your body. The first time, it can be quite a physical and emotional jolt. Very quickly, however, your cells get used to it, integrating the power and recognizing this as your new norm.

There is no right way to get this. Whatever happens is perfect, even if it is nothing. In fact, some people have quite a delayed reaction, getting nothing at the time but having big breakthroughs or clarity that night, or during the next week. Even if you never feel anything from this, trust that your soul is following your intention to harmonize and align all parts of you into a higher state. It is what it is.

I had a cute experience doing a Fusion on my eight year-old nephew Lukas. First I did Soul Body Fusion on his mother, my sister Maureen. She was having major surgery the next day and wanted "a little extra support." She felt nothing but a little movement in her stomach. However, she later admitted that she "vibrated all night long." Since Lukas was curious, I asked him if he wanted to try. We were sitting outside, so he hopped up on a patio chair. His little legs didn't touch the ground, so we found a box on which to rest his feet. Eight-year-old boys aren't big on spiritual theory, so I quickly explained that we were going to bring more of his light or energy into his body. I asked him to put his palms up and explained that I would touch his fingertips for a few minutes. He could close his eyes and tell me what he felt.

I immediately saw his eyelids flicker. Within ten seconds of my gently touching his hands, one of his legs started twitching and his arms began to shake. He popped open his big blue eyes and exclaimed: "That's not me!"

"It's okay," I reassured him. "That's just the energy coming in."

His arms and leg continued to shake as he asked me for clarity: "Now I'm supposed to think about bringing in my inner god, right?" I smiled warmly at the wisdom and innocence of his words. He looked angelic, sitting in the sun with eyes closed, drinking in his personal god. It was only another minute or two before Lukas was again wide-eyed: "I see so many lights and colors moving around! I can't keep my eyes closed!"

"That's okay," I answered. "Just tell me what you see."

"Black-and-white zebra stripes turned to bright white. Now it's all green!" With that Lukas was done, saying flatly, "I can't do this anymore because the chair keeps shaking too much."

Can you see that this child had no expectations? What happened was a true and pure experience of the alignment into his body of higher frequencies of light.

Physical Changes

The Soul Body Fusion impacts your body at many levels, resulting in rapid clearings or openings on each of the physical, emotional, and spiritual planes. You will notice that some of these examples are from people who experienced a Fusion by phone, by video, over the internet, or from a friend or practitioner at a distance. It is wonderful how distance is no object.

Carolina in Sweden reported: "It blew my mind! For the first nine minutes I felt the energy moving. Suddenly it felt like the Tetris game—every little piece fell into my body in perfect order! I felt so BIG! And every part of me was perfect! I am whole!"

Karen felt immediate changes on a physical level within minutes during a Fusion with me on the phone. She felt energy and heat moving around her body. She exclaimed: "An old car accident injury just came out of my neck! I briefly felt the accident and the blow pushing my neck inward. Now I feel the physical trauma pulled out of my neck! I need to stand. My feet feel like they are really, really stuck to Earth. I'm walking around, trying to get used to how it feels to be in my body. I'm feeling lots of energy and movement in my knee. It's now working on an old knee surgery."

Monica shared her excitement about the physical impact: "My body is clearing out and losing weight. So much changed! I think this is a way of changing the world!"

Berit, from Stockholm, wrote this about her phone Fusion:

> *For the first two or three minutes nothing happened. Then my breathing raced. My body started to move in chaotic and wild ways. It was like fireworks going off inside me! I stood up and danced.*
>
> *Suddenly I was filled with bubbling joy! After I finished the call, my body felt so light and free, and at the same time I felt so deeply healed. Lying down, I realized I was still vibrating. Not shaking so that you could see, but extreme vibration inside. Waking up, I felt wonder and a strong feeling of presence in my body. I am left with deep gratitude.*

Emotional Changes

For some, SBF is a life makeover. People progress from fears and limitations to living with a soul-infused personality. A retired teacher went home after her Fusion and started to throw out all her old clothes. She said, "Now I will start a new life!"

Kathleen had a lot to say about the impact of a Fusion on her life:

> *The SBF has opened new doors for me… doors I never even knew existed. For the first time ever I experience myself as pure innocence; every deed is purely driven by love!! Laughter has been my companion as I realized that I am what I have spent a lifetime trying to be. The Soul Body Fusion technology has allowed me to see that I already am heaven (my soul) on earth (my body). My self image has shifted from weak human to amazingly empowered divine messenger… just an astounding experience!*

Mats, in Norway, explains his emotional release during an SBF workshop:

> *Rather immediately I felt pain in my lower back and solar plexus. Also, I was losing power. I started to cry and bent forward. I felt that the root of the pain was from a situation when I was an eight-year-old boy: It was spring and the stream was flooding when I and two other boys, Peter and Tony, were playing with bark boats. We weren't allowed to be by the stream, and it was quite far from home as well. Tony's boat got stuck by the shore, and he tried to release it with a stick but fell in and was swept away by the waves. We ran after him and tried to rescue him but couldn't. Tony drowned*

that day. Something died in me as well. My joy and trust in my parents. No explanations, no debriefing or deeper understanding. Not allowed to talk about it.

The second time we received a Fusion in the class I traveled down to my lower back. The pain was there, but in a very short time a white/golden light went down there, bringing a feeling of relief. The white/golden light took the form of an image of Tony's face. He said, or told me telepathically, that I had to forgive myself. He had never been angry with me, as I had always thought. The pain disappeared and I cried again, this time in grateful respect. I can really feel that something changed and healed the old memory, both in body and mind.

Jenny is a young single mother, a new Colombian immigrant to Denmark. She came to a Soul Body Fusion class after a single session from an SBF practitioner that changed her life:

I was depressed, jealous, angry, and isolated. I have a ten-year-old son and was with an aggressive, abusive boyfriend. After a while I got sick too. I didn't trust myself or anyone else. Finally, it got to be too much, so I took my son and left my boyfriend. My friend Monica did SBF on me, and many things happened! I got my soul grounded and my personality changed 90 percent! It is now very easy for me to control myself and focus again. My son is different too: more patient, calm, grounded—easier to manage. Even my boyfriend changed, and we weren't living together! He doesn't know why. The light that now enlightens me is making others around me feel peaceful and happy, seeking my help. Every cell of my body can feel it, multi-dimensionally. I am the light. I finally broke out of the box and am free to be the real Jenny!

When Jenny shared her story to the class, we were all reaching for tissues at the magnitude of the change in her, her son, and her abusive relationship. I asked, "How long did it take after the SBF session for these changes to occur?" Astonishingly, she answered, "I had a 180-degree change in my life immediately. This all changed in a minute."

For many, the grounding and integration that takes place during a Fusion creates immediate shifts in their lives. Kirsten in Denmark had this experience:

At the Soul Body Fusion course I realized my soul was only integrated down to my solar plexus, and my legs were like the legs of a rag doll—no real grounding or strength. I was easily knocked over, and I found it difficult to stand my ground. Now I am more at home in myself, finding my balance quickly. My strength has been challenged by some who were provoked by my new energy. I have worked through this and released the anger, which has increased my personal power. I have more flow, so jobs and money are coming my way. I see things clearer, with more depth. My understanding has expanded and I feel I have been lifted to a higher state.

Spiritual Changes

Reina, now one of our Certified Soul Body Fusion teachers, wrote about her initial experience after a one day workshop: "I started my spiritual path when I was twenty-seven years old and had my first out-of-body experience then. I've been working my butt off ever since, looking for my joy. I found it here in one afternoon!"

Solveig, a twenty-year-old from Denmark clearly describes the difficulty of so many people who have a strong angelic component in their soul and have never really felt at home here on Earth.

> *Sometimes I don't see the world through my own eyes but more out of a pair of eyes in my forehead, or even above my head. I don't want to have this feeling of light in the upper part of my body, while the lower part feels dark and dead. I need my heavenly spirit to come down in my legs and feet and continue down into the earth, creating a strong safety line to pull me down as a counter-weight to the strong power that seems to be pulling me up toward heaven. After the Soul Body Fusion class, I feel stronger. I am no longer fragile—not so afraid of the world and my gifts as before. The best part of all is—my heart doesn't hurt anymore!*

Mary K. wrote this about the spiritual aspects of her experience: "During the distant Soul Body Fusion sessions, I felt like spiritual "Liquid Plumber" was really working hard to clear my heart chakra. It was powerful, consistent, steady energy—more powerful yet in the same steady vein as Reiki or other spiritual healing. It is my impression that it was delivering the potential for multidimensional consciousness. I believe the wonderful Soul Body Fusion sessions unlocked some unknown potential in me."

Paola received the Fusion by listening to me do an internet radio broadcast:

> *It was absolutely beautiful and amazing! I've been doing a lot of work on my own consciousness, and I now real-*

ize—and it seems so obvious—that I was not living my divinity from inside my own physical body! In the first phase, I had the sensation and awareness of energy moving, melding, and merging into my body. In the second phase, there was this divine light coming through. I feel more centered now, whereas before I didn't want to be inside my own body, thinking that to experience divinity as a human, my mind needed to be in the higher realms. Thank you!

Making it Stick

Is this permanent? Yes, although a huge trauma could cause you to lose some of your alignment. To help the body synthesize the changes, White Eagle suggests that you repeat the process two more times following the initial Fusion. The first repetition is one week later. Leave a two-week gap and then do a third Fusion. The final process will be three weeks after your initial experience.

I see Soul Body Fusion as an iterative process. The initial Fusion can bring significant clearing at all levels. Vesa, a Finnish man in his early thirties, emailed me about his experience in an SBF course: "I had a huge cleaning after a Fusion as toxins came out. It rebooted my nervous system. It was hard to manage the energy, because it was so high. Slept less but had lots of extra energy."

Over the three-week period your body, your personality, your life shifts to accommodate the new, improved you. Another reason we do it three times over three weeks is that for some people, very little appears to happen at first. Their biggest shifts occur in the second or third week. New levels of light penetrate your resistances and work on deeper growth at each

Fusion. One gentleman laughed during his first session. The second week he tapped into deep sorrow.

Don't worry if you forget to do the follow-up Fusions exactly one week and three weeks later. Do the best you can. You may notice that these subsequent Fusions are quicker. Remember? No Rules. For instance, five minutes per phase may feel perfect for you. I still encourage you to do the follow-up processes in two phases, with at least a minute break between them.

It Keeps Processing

Soul Body Fusion creates a permanent change and opens up an endless, often nonlinear process of growth. After the first three weeks, the changes may not be as noticeable. Personally, when I do a Fusion on myself, I never feel more than a little cellular tingling and perhaps a deep sense of joy. The majority of times I don't feel anything. Does this mean that nothing is happening? Certainly not. Once the big changes at the physical and emotional levels settle in, the higher levels of soul changes are finer and more subtle. I trust that higher and lighter dimensions of my being are continually being harmonized into my body. I suggest you do the same. We can't see our own growth. My best feedback comes from friends who don't see me often. They tell me: "You're different, more solid, more in your power." Or they might comment on my radiance or the energy they sense around me. Sometimes people report spontaneous Fusions occurring anytime after their initial experience.

The best proof of Soul Body Fusion isn't how intense your reaction is; it is how your life changes. Here are some improvements you may notice over the longer term: better diet and health, better balance, improved commitment to exercise, more energy, more clarity of mission, more confidence, better body image, healed relationships, healed patterns and trauma, greater abundance. Others report they've gained new qualities: they are more flexible and fluid, more magnetic to good, more intuitive, less stressed, more empowered, happier, more accepting, looking and feeling younger.

Here are examples from two people whose major changes came after all three Fusions:

Reina, USA

Since my last Soul Body Fusion there has been this rock of Gibraltar energy within me—soul— immovable, immutable, unassailable. And it just sits there, vibrating powerfully. I can no longer do things the way I used to. This vibrating truth resonates such powerful clarity that I am unable to do anything that doesn't match this frequency. Parts of me feel I "should" do things; however, there is no way I can. Truth just sits there, showing me that the only reason I'm doing it is out of responsibility and fear. No chocolate either! Bummer—doesn't match the new resonance. This clarity isn't being forced on me—it is just powerfully there, way beyond words. It is powerful, unavoidable knowing.

Dani, USA

The Soul Body Fusion process has changed my life. After the third Fusion I noticed a significant change in my awareness. I felt my body responding and supporting my intuitive soul nature. It felt different to be able to feel, hear, and experience the harmony. There is an added clarity to my path; having the body and soul work together to guide me is so powerful. It adds confidence to each step.

Soul Body Fusion is so simple it's easy to take for granted. Berdine in the Netherlands told me: "The changes are never huge for me. But when I think back, I notice that I look at things in a different way. I do things differently. Things are internalizing. For instance, now when I meditate, everything happens inside me. I don't have to go outside myself to change the world."

After the first three SBF sessions over three weeks, you can continue to do Fusions on yourself as often as you like. There is no end to the spiritual growth and integration that is possible. However, your experiences may become increasingly subtle. When I do Fusions for friends, family and the world, I often add my own intention for a Fusion into the mix.

Consider the potential of what is happening. Here is a process in which you don't *do* anything, yet amazing shifts occur! When you remove the effort you're left with grace. It works on all levels. In many cases, it enables healing; it accelerates personal and spiritual growth. It takes no skill and little time. There are no downside risks or side effects. Because your soul is in charge, and it is infinitely wiser than your personality, even if your body's reaction is difficult, there can be no harm. There is no healer; there is no interference by anyone. If a person "does" Soul Body Fusion on you, that person is partnering with you to set an intention and hold a high resonant field. What's the catch? The only catch I can come up with is that it requires us to believe in something that seems quite unbelievable. This is a tool that comes from a new paradigm, a new energy world. So you have nothing to lose and much to gain by giving it a try.

An Illumination Visualization

What follows is a brief channeled meditation to help you feel the bliss and light of the Soul Body Fusion:

Be welcomed now as sun and body. Feel the code of lights within your body lift so you can ascend. Arise with your body and your light to a temple of light, where you are received and welcomed. There are changes taking place within you to enable this journey. Some of you may see, and others will feel or know. Much of this is beyond your ability to visualize, but each of you with your enlightened body is received in this higher dimensional temple.

You have many masters who have been guides and guardians of your soul's journey. They are with you now, helping to organize your frequencies. You may feel nothing, as this is higher than your awareness now knows how to go. But you are learning quickly.

Divinity and humanity are fusing here, creating a new material, recreating matter. The DNA in your cells is responding. Remember to breathe and expand. Feel yourself as whole and holy. Feel an inner radiation, an inner light glowing from your cells. Feel your aura shift to encompass this inner illumination.

Imagine yourself as an illumined one—one who trusts, who listens, who magnetizes only goodness, who radiates only goodness. Imagine now the changes large and small in your life that you are opening to receive. Let nothing hold the inner illumination back. Let it be.

Let not your fears or your plans limit the inner light of your divinity.

Move past your own individual experience now and feel the luminous, transcendent quality of the higher group consciousness of which you are a part. Be aware of the aliveness, the intelligence, and the wisdom of this group consciousness and light. It becomes stronger as your awareness expands.

As your awareness of this high group consciousness stabilizes, move your attention to human consciousness, feeling its illumination and its potential. Feel this high group that you are a part of sending illumination through the gridwork of humanity, through the web of human souls.

Feel the light welcoming you home!

Chapter 6

Doing Soul Body Fusion with Another

I love Soul Body Fusion—it's the best thing I have ever learned—so simple and so effective!

-Tove, Norway

Working in Pairs

Now that you've experienced receiving a Soul Body Fusion on your own, it's time to try it with a partner. Anyone is eligible. Let's start with humans; later we'll talk about doing Fusions on animals and even places and situations. First, you'll practice in person. Later, you can extend this to using the process with someone who is geographically remote.

Over the years I've come up with an easy method to work with a partner. Put two chairs close together so that you and your partner are facing. Get close enough that you can easily put your hands on your partner's hands without straining or stretching. If possible, I put my legs outside my partner's so I am creating a perimeter, or a safe space. Explain what you'll be doing, without saying too much about what to expect. Of course, it may be helpful to share *your* experience and what the benefits have been for you. It may also be interesting to ask your partner, "What do you think the soul is?"

Jonette demonstrating a paired Fusion. Fig. 6.1

Follow the same guidelines as you did on yourself. The process is nonlinear; it isn't controlled by you or the recipient. While there are many variations, for facilitators the basics include the following: set an intention, ask their soul to guide the process, let go and relax, notice changes, ask for feedback.

1. Set the intention

Either one or both of you can state the intention aloud. Here is an example: "It is our intention that [fill in the name] permanently aligns and harmonizes [his/her] physical body with the highest vibration of [his /her] soul's light that is possible at this time." Use whatever words are comfortable for the recipient.

2. Assume a position with feet on the floor – their palms up, yours down

Have your partner sit, hands on lap, palms up. You will place your palms down, lightly covering your partner's fingers with your fingers. Please don't cover the palms, as they are important chakras for receiving the energy. Feel free to rest your wrists on your partner's knees. In the Soul Body Fusion process we indicate "receiving" by open hands, palms up. We indicate "giving" by turning our palms down. Our downturned hand is modeling our intention to help bring our partner's higher energies all the way through the legs and feet into the ground.

3. Stay present and grounded

Remind your partner to stay present in the body. Both of you need to be alert, not drift off or meditate. Your job is to feel connected to the other, stay focused, solid, and present.

4. Observe the experience, don't judge or analyze

Remind your partner that his or her higher self knows exactly what to do, how to do it, and when. Neither the facilitator, nor the person receiving the Fusion should push, force, or fix anything. Carefully witness what is happening.

Suggest to your partner to drink water before, during, and after the process. You drink too, as your own Fusion will get stronger as you sit and hold the space for someone else. You may notice that after a minute or two you can't really tell which of you is getting the Fusion. It isn't a one-way street. You together become immersed in one combined, high, harmonized field that brings both of you to a higher vibration. I find that I "get" a Fusion every time I "give" one. Who wouldn't want that?

Soul Body Fusion is not a linear transmission of healing energies. It works at a quantum level. The source is everywhere. Your intention, like a prayer, materializes it.

Nothing goes from you into the other person except the influence of your resonant field. You are not interfering in any way with the other's energy, body, or karma. You help support your partner to hold a high space and strengthen the intention. Remember, your partner's soul is in charge of everything that happens during the process and after. When I teach SBF I often have students repeat after me, "I can't mess it up because I'm not doing anything anyway!" When I do a Fusion, I don't explain much, if anything, ahead of time about what to expect, so as to not color the experience. Later, in the sharing, I just listen and respond with "okay," or "good."

Phase One: Ten Minutes

For approximately ten minutes, sit facing your partner as described above. Your partner should feel free to have closed eyes, but not to nap or meditate. You may close yours too. There is no problem if either of you wants to keep your eyes open; however, it may be more distracting. The task of the person receiving Soul Body Fusion is to observe any changes or feelings. It's okay if your partner remains quiet the entire ten minutes and reports any experiences during the break, or he or she can share the experiences as the Fusion progresses. It's fine if your partner doesn't notice any changes at all. Remember my first Fusion? I didn't feel a thing, so I asked for confirmation to come from outside.

A helpful analogy is that of recharging a car with a low battery. You hook up the cables—with one end connected to the low battery, the other connected to a strong battery in a running car. It only takes a few minutes for the charge to reignite the low battery. Once the car is going strong, the connection is no longer needed. You are simply jump-starting the other person to a higher level of power and alignment.

If your partner has a strong experience, you may want to remove your hands, perhaps even move your chair back to allow more energetic space. It isn't required that you touch your partner for the full ten minutes. In fact, with remote Fusions, which we will discuss later in this chapter, there is no touching at all.

Take a Break

After ten minutes, remove your hands and perhaps slide your chair back a bit. Drink water. Talk over what the receiver experienced and share what you may have noticed, mainly focusing on the receiver. Be accepting of whatever is shared, as there is no right or wrong experience. If there was no feeling, help the person understand that this is the beginning of a process and it can take days or weeks, or there may never be any physical changes.

Phase Two: Ten Minutes

After the break, pull your chairs together again and resume the position with hands touching. Continue holding the intention for the Fusion. Do this for another ten minutes or so. Remember, talking is fine. You both should focus on feeling solid, grounded, and observant. It is important that the practitioner and the receiver merely witness what is happening without pushing or fixing. If there is an imbalance or an adjustment is needed, observe the need and then let it go. Not doing anything is the key that allows the direction to be set from a higher dimension. The experience in the second ten minutes may be quite different from the first phase. Trust the process. The results are more wondrous and unexpected than we can predict.

When I first practiced Fusions on others, I diligently used my clairvoyance and healing skills to see what was happening and to help remove blocks and move the energy around. I've come to learn that the less I do; the more that happens for my partner. I am constantly surprised that I can hold hands with someone for ten minutes, feeling and doing nothing, and that person reports amazing shifts! I simply concentrate on being connected and on our joint intention for a Soul Body Fusion.

When It's Done
If the person receiving Soul Body Fusion didn't talk about the experience during the process, ask now what was felt. Some questions you might ask are:

- How was this phase different from the first phase?
- How does your body feel overall?
- What happened in your hands and feet?
- What, if any, emotional shifts did you feel?

I am always pleased to hear comments about shifts in the feet because those indicate that the cellular changes went all the way down. Often people have physical sensations in the hands, arms, head, and upper body at first, and only in the second ten minutes does it begin to move past the hips into the legs and feet. It is a sign that their higher energies are fully grounding into them.

Soul Body Fusion can be a powerful tool in healing the effects that led people to separate their spirit from their body in the first place. Examples: eating disorders, abuse of all kinds, psychological issues, abandonment, stress, violence, and feelings of unworthiness.

A caveat for those of you with clairvoyant or healing gifts: even though you may see or sense what is going on with your partner or get relevant messages, please do not share any of this until the Fusion is completed. Your well-meaning insights take the focus away from observing how the soul works. After the Fusion, feel free to say what you learned or noticed.

Possible Reactions

Most of the time people feel great after the Fusion. They report being more solidly in their body than ever before: "It was like sinking into an old, soft, comfortable chair—and the chair was my body," one woman commented. Another kept stroking the skin of her arms, saying, "I've never really felt my body before." They talk of finally "being home." They feel powerful, light, energized, clear, in love with themselves, glowing, and happy.

Overall, approximately 90 percent feel some sort of physical or emotional sensation during the Fusion process. About 60 percent feel heat, tingling, vibrations, or pressure. I find it interesting that roughly 70 percent feel the Fusion begin in their head and move down their body. For others it may start in their arms, their feet, their heart area, or the top and bottom simultaneously. For many the physical shift feels electrical, like cellular rewiring to prepare the nervous system for a higher frequency. Deidre in Denmark described her experience: "A rod of light went through the top of my head and down my spine. Then my head opened up and pressure came down and light came up out of me to meet it. Then everything merged." Kelly put it this way: "I have never felt energy like that pass through my body!"

Since the body needs time to integrate the electricity of the higher vibrations, you don't want to interfere by touching or hugging at the end. I suggest quiet time if possible. The body is amazing in its ability to reformat itself to higher frequencies. Within minutes the more dramatic reactions will stop and people will begin to adjust.

Uncomfortable Reactions

People's reactions are not always sweetness and light. During or following the process some may feel sick, achy, or tired. Advise them to drink water and to rest. Cells have purged toxins and undergone changes. Sometimes a person may get a slight fever and have flu like symptoms for a day. Celebrate these shifts! Every feeling heralds the opening of something once stuck in the body.

Gro, who learned SBF at a workshop in Norway, didn't have a strong personal experience at all. Nevertheless, in the spirit of experimentation, she went home that evening and tried it on her unsuspecting husband. Within a moment he became hot and asked if she had just turned up the heat. "I'm burning up," he said.

"No," she calmly replied and continued touching his hands. A moment later he exclaimed, agitated, "What are you doing? Stop! I'm feeling sick!" Evidently the higher energy frequencies of his spirit came in so quickly and powerfully that it resulted in his feeling nauseated. If something like this happens for you, remove your hands. The person has probably had enough. Always, always use your intuition as a guide. Feel free to ask for feedback so your partner can tap also into his or her own intuitive wisdom.

On a few occasions the energies of soul alignment are so strong that people have experienced significant pressure or pain around their heart or a more rapid heartbeat. One woman swore she was having a heart attack, even though the Soul Body Fusion practitioner insisted that it was only the Fusion opening her heart. She went to the hospital for tests and found nothing whatsoever was wrong with her heart. I feel confident that even in cases where there are physical or emotional discomforts, there can be no harm. The entire premise is that their soul is the driving force, not you.

One woman, who received her Fusion while watching me demonstrate to an audience of many hundreds, described her somewhat painful experience as "hard docking." The metaphor is of a space shuttle crashing into the space station rather than gently coming together with it when docking. "I was hysterical for half an hour as every emotion crowded in and flowed out." She gives some advice if this happens to you: "Use your breath. Water helps—both internally and externally—baths or showers. Call on help to balance the energy. Go with the flow. Don't be surprised if you shake intermittently, shiver, and feel hot and cold at the same time. You may have wandering aches and pains, muscle cramps, and spasms. On the other hand, there is a brand-new sense of balance evolving, a sense of new potentials there to be chosen."

Anne had a spontaneous Soul Body Fusion months after she first started doing Fusions on herself and others:

> *I was with Jonette and a group of friends, doing some channeling and meditations together. I suddenly felt weak, like I was losing all the power in my body. I called out to my friends for support, as I was frightened. I grew weaker and weaker, as if all my electricity was pulled out from my feet. After a while I was an empty body, like a shell. It was such a strange feeling. I asked Jonette and the others for a special Soul Body Fusion. Jonette held my feet, and together we pulled new energy into and through me. When we were done, I felt a new electrical system in my body, much stronger than the old one—a total transfusion. I think it was an upgraded SBF, that I was rewired electrically to prepare me for a special trip later that year.*

Follow-up

Soul Body Fusion is an on-going process. As you did with yourself, it is best to do two more Fusions over the next three weeks. It is great if you can actually meet with your partner one week later, and then three weeks later to do the follow-up Fusions. If not possible in person, use the phone or internet. If neither of these options is open, do the Fusion on the appropriate days by sitting with palms down and visualizing your partner receiving into upturned hands.

Can you do a Fusion on someone more often than the three times I mention in the guidelines? Yes! Because there is a continuous possibility for growth and because the soul or higher self will make sure not to give more than he or she can handle. Again, use your intuition or simply ask your partner what he or she feels is best. Can you do just one session and no follow-up? That's okay too. Do what you can. Of course, one session is always better than none; however, three sessions are optimal.

Step by Step

What follows are transcripts of two Soul Body Fusions demonstrations I did in front of a class. I used them as a training example; therefore, I utilized my clairvoyance while asking the volunteers to narrate what they felt. We demonstrated only the first ten-minute phase. Please note that being clairvoyant, seeing visions, or being sensitive to what is happening to the recipient is not a requirement for success in facilitating Fusions.

Jacque
JONETTE (placing her hands on Jacque's hands, talking to the class): It is our intention that starts the process. I focus on her

soul's vibration and see that it's very, very high. Once I connect to it, I ask to connect to her physical vibration, and then hold both in my awareness.

JACQUE: I'm feeling a lot of swirling, entwining energy and seeing golden speckles in my crown chakra. A feeling of metal or something heavy is over my shoulders—a good feeling, but there is weight, like hair flowing over my shoulders. My heart chakra is opening and I feel my chakras aligning.

JONETTE: There is some rigidity. I'm drawn to the back of the spinal column. I notice less energy at the back of her heart. I often notice that people have shields at the back of their heart. It is where we protect ourselves. Now I feel her heart can open the gate and more of her soul is coming in. What is happening to your legs and feet?

JACQUE: The right side feels lighter and there's darkness on the left side.

JONETTE: Hold both of them in your awareness until both take on the greater light. I feel a shift from front to back and side to side.

JACQUE: It feels like my right foot is several inches off the floor.

JONETTE: The body will balance itself. If one-half of the body is stronger, hold the intention that the weaker side recalibrates to the power of the stronger. You don't need to do anything else.

JACQUE: It feels like a settling-out process.

JONETTE: I can say that as a facilitator, you may feel something happening in your own body. It doesn't mean you're taking something on; it means that your body is communicating and receiving information from the other person.

Jacque may believe that she needs a foot in both worlds. I sense now that there is a bit of blockage at her lower back as another level of stuckness reveals itself.

JACQUE: I'm feeling a lot around my heart and it feels like I need to cough.

JONETTE: She is experiencing a changing electrical system so that her soul can fully inhabit her body all of the time. Our souls automatically want to do this. It's a gentle process. You don't need to know how to do it. Just sit there with the clear intention.

JACQUE: Something very subtle is going on at my crown. My feet have almost settled down.

JONETTE: As the higher vibrations come in we have to give up our fear of our power. I feel there was a big energy transfer just now. The new circuitry is done and now the energy of the higher aspects of her soul can move in. It is a process of opening up the energy meridians and inviting the soul in. It's not complete when we're done touching hands. It is a continuing process. It feels complete for now, but it's not over.

JACQUE: It feels like twinkling Christmas lights or like bubbling champagne.

JONETTE: Sometimes the vibrational changes are so much that you may not want to hug or touch the other for about an hour or so. Congratulate her. Her field is now bright and open. Thank you.

Christopher
CHRIS: As a child I was encouraged not to show emotions. I was told things like "Don't be too happy."

JONETTE: Your emotions therefore don't know where to roost in your body, because it wasn't okay to register positive or negative emotions. The electrical system doesn't know what to do. Intend that your electrical system be okay with owning your feelings and have that open up the pathways so the meridians can heal themselves. That will allow you to let your guard down and regain your emotional flow. Relax and disengage. The spirit of intention will do it all. Your mind doesn't want to trust. Take that away and relax. Now there is an opening up and an unwinding of the energies going on. The biggest block to your soul is that you don't feel safe being who you are. Be with the essence that "I am safe. I am safe. I am safe." What are you feeling now?

CHRIS: My ego is like an over devoted nurse—always checking on the baby.

JONETTE: I'm sensing that we have to unravel the knotted up coils of your energy meridians. You can't put more light in until they're straightened. Please try to ease that hyper vigilance. Relax. I can't even see the meridians, they are so tight. I'm going to wait until I see them unwinding.

CHRIS: My ego is waiting to say that this isn't going to work. My higher self is saying, "I let my light shine." Then the ego responds, "What are you? Nuts?" [He begins speaking to the resistance.] "I know how to use my power appropriately for the benefit of all. It is my right to allow my light to shine."

JONETTE: Please get away from words now and allow the circuitry to repair. Now we can ask your soul to come in more fully. Continue to open up your electrical system to allow in more of your greatness.

CHRIS: I feel a lot of twitching in my heart, hands, solar plexus, spine, soles of my feet, and my thighs feel weak.

JONETTE: You have a really bright heart, but it felt as if it was in a cage. Feel the bars disintegrating. Allow those twitches to happen, because it is enabling the cells to continue igniting each other.

CHRIS: I saw a vision of a large, pink dragon coming out of my heart. I was looking at him, and he winked and is now stretching and nuzzling my face.

JONETTE: Allow him to merge with you. The dragon is often a symbol of large transformation. He's waking you up. Let him bring his power into you.

CHRIS: He's sitting in a cockpit, playing with the controls. He says I'm acclimatizing, that I'm hurting from being cramped for so long.

JONETTE: Let the cage open up. Intend that your soul moves more into your body. Visualize your cells purging impurities. Let your cells be more flexible and more plumped up as you take in more light. See your ego observing and notice that your ego is coming along too.

CHRIS: My ego has agreed to observe and not to control. Light and dark energy are swirling around each other. I feel lightness and heaviness in the same space.

JONETTE: Allow them to balance out. It's not really dark; it's tarnished. Imagine enzymes going to work on the tarnish.

CHRIS: I'm waiting for effervescence. There is a feeling of it in my forearms. My body feels much more alive.

JONETTE: Put more consciousness in your legs and feet so that they feel the aliveness too. Intend that this wash into you [Chris burps—a good indicator of changes]. Check in on the dragon. What is he doing?

CHRIS: He's doing a systems check. He's busy with his work.

JONETTE: Command him to pay attention to you. Have him face you again. Feel the power he reminds you that you have. He only deals with equals, not those who are weaker. He is you and not outside of you. He's a part of your power that you feel. He's now as big as the metropolitan area. Trust.

CHRIS: He's back into me.

JONETTE: It looks like that is how he's going to merge. Feel that. The dragon symbolizes your soul energy. It was captive in your heart. Your heart was huge because it always had so much potential. When your heart energy finally got unblocked, it opened up the energy meridians in your body. This will allow any emotions that come forth to finally flow and be released.

Debrief of the Examples

You will notice that in the demonstrations with Jacque and Chris I took an active part in dialoging with them during the process. This is easy for me because I've been an intuitive healer for decades. It also helps me better explain the process to a class. Don't think for a minute that *you* have to be able to sense what is happening to the other person or direct that person's attention. Soul Body Fusion works simply because you are connecting in service and holding the intention, not because you have some special skill or gifts. What I love about this is that it is so simple—no rituals, required belief systems, no levels or degrees. Everything flows from your heartfelt connection, clear intention and from the fact that we are meant to embody our spirit.

Remote Fusions

Just as you can do a Fusion facing each other and touching hands, so can you do it remotely. Time and space do not separate consciousness. As in Reiki, prayer, or other distance healing, nothing is lost if your partner and you are on opposite sides of the world. I most often do Fusions over the phone. Take, for example, Beth. I give her the same instructions as if she were in front of me. I sit with my palms down, exactly as if I had my hands on hers. After jointly setting our intention, we put the phone down or turn on the speaker for ten minutes while I do the first phase of the Fusion. Then we pick up the phone again and share. Next we repeat the process for another ten minutes, and finally talk about the results. Follow your intuition—the ten minutes is only a guideline. I do it longer if it feels like we're in the middle of a major shift. On some occasions I'm drawn to do three phases instead of two.

Similar to in-person Fusion sessions, the remote process is strengthened if you do it three times over three weeks. A week after the first Fusion, sit quietly with your palms down and visualize a second Fusion with your partner. I usually find this is quicker and I still suggest doing two phases. I spend between five and fifteen minutes total connecting with my client remotely, intending for the Fusion to continue to strengthen in that period. Because time and distance are irrelevant in these cosmic connections, there is no need to synchronize the transmission times. However, the client will get a clearer experience of the shifts by sitting sometime that day for five to fifteen minutes with palms up, intending to connect to you and the process. Do the same a third time, three weeks from the initial Fusion. Again, don't worry if you miss the exact date. Do the best you can.

If I've taught a Soul Body Fusion class on a particular weekend, I do a group Fusion the next week by imagining the entire class receiving another Fusion together. I don't focus on them specifically or even recall their names.

Results from Remote Fusions

As I've mentioned before, Fusions work in all kinds of remote situations, including by video transmission. Here are some examples:

Reina, USA

> *I have used SBF with my folks remotely and I can see a significant change, especially in my dad. He has taken up gardening after making fun of my mom for forty years. He loves it. He is more open, loving, and supportive. It is very gratifying, as my dad is a PhD engineer and very data oriented. He used to have the arrogance that goes along with this. The arrogance has softened. More of his heart is available.*

Gloria, Colombia

> *It is evident that this was the most intense long distance healing I have experienced. At first, I felt a strong, intense energy on my right eye. Afterward, it was as if a*

whole medical staff was working in my heart. When the session ended, I was shocked, stirred, frightened, and at the same time happy, with a peaceful tranquility. I slept profoundly. Then my daily routine got totally out of hand: I didn't meet deadlines, left chores undone, didn't take care of things.

Miracles have happened in my life since the third SBF session. The chaotic energy moving all around, the first days, has settled into a new, innovative way of organizing my surroundings and affairs. My closest relationships are improving, getting harmonious. My room is now in order, and I am organizing everything in a most surprising way. My perception and intuition are showing up—my intuition had been stored on the shelf for forty four years. Things and experiences are taken care of with ease, and I welcome patience! SBF is a valuable tool for our ascension and union between matter and spirit.

Grant, Canada

While watching the video I began to experience intense feelings of joy centered around my heart chakra. Over the next few weeks I watched it again and again and experienced the same sense of overwhelming joy. I should also mention that for the past few weeks since then I've experienced alternating periods of joy and anger. This morning I woke up with a sense of joy so extreme that it borders on being uncomfortable. It is now 1:30p.m. and I've been feeling extremely joyful since waking. Now, you may think this would be a really good thing; however, feeling this sense of joy for such an extended period of time does take a little getting used to.

Johanna, Germany

> *I did the videos on the website. After a few days I had more than four shifts in my energy flows. With a tender "thud" I landed in my own heart. I feel my Divine Being and balance also. Since then, I AM that I AM in a very new and also wonderful, confident, and beneficial way! It was a multidimensional healing—past, present, and future— healing all fractals of my being.*

Linda, USA

> *I have done two Soul Body Fusions from the video on the website. Since then my life has taken a very different turn. Some days I am not "me" anymore. My ego is separating from my authentic self in a loving, gentle way. Insights come to me daily; urges are diminishing that once held me. I follow through on ideas and take action. I have greater self-worth. My goal has been to find peace within myself, and it feels like the door has finally opened.*

Jan's First Fusion

Jan from Idaho shares one of the most striking examples of the power of Soul Body Fusion, even over a distance. Jan's friend John was involuntarily hospitalized on suicide watch.

> *I had just finished the Soul Body Fusion course on CDs when I got a phone call that a friend, John, was suicidal. I thought, "Here's my chance to practice Soul Body Fusion!" I did Fusions on him all night long. Whenever I thought about it, I'd do another one.*

I saw him about three days later. I had not seen him look this good for about three years. Here are his words: "I don't know what happened! I'm happy! I feel free! I can think! I can love! I'm more tolerant of other peoples' ideas of what the world is about. I like being in the presence of others. I'm looking through new eyes! I'm thinking with my heart! I have lost all my feelings of fear!"

Weeks later I called and asked him to describe what happened. He said, "Prior to the Soul Body Fusion, I couldn't think; I couldn't put two thoughts together. I was angry all the time, blaming other people. I couldn't emote. I couldn't feel anyone else's feelings. I woke up every day afraid. I was placed in the hospital under suicide watch because I felt like this was the way I would be for the rest of my life. I had lost my identity, my intellect. I had no life."

When you see him, there is nothing of the old person left. He is just light. He wants to hug everyone and tell everyone how wonderful the world is! This was my very first time trying Soul Body Fusion, so I expect big things to come!

It is incredible to realize that Jan had just learned the Fusion process from a CD course. She had never received a Soul Body Fusion herself. She had never tried it on anyone before. She did the process at a distance. Perhaps most amazing: her friend didn't even know that she was doing anything! This shows that it is the facilitator's intention that is so important. John went from severely depressed and suicidal to open, glowing, and happy in a few hours!

Asking Permission

This brings us to another question that often comes up: "How can I do something on someone else without first asking for permission?" Let's look deeply at that question. First, with Soul Body Fusion you aren't doing anything. You are setting an intention that invites someone's spirit to align more completely. Any change is carried out by the soul. Second, are you ultimately really separate from someone else? Aren't other people just manifestations of the divine, as are you? Third, whose permission would you ask? Their ego or personality self? Is that really them? It is the false paradigm of separation that holds us back from truly helping others in every way possible. The true paradigm is oneness. So my perspective is that for this, no permission is needed. If you are uncomfortable with this idea, let your higher self ask permission from their higher self.

The Sky Is the Limit

If Soul Body Fusion works one-on-one in person and one-on–one remotely, why not do Fusions on whole groups? You don't have to ask permission. They don't have to know you are doing something. Consider that almost all limits are self-generated. I've done Fusions on YouTube, on internet radio broadcasts, in front of audiences. It works!

Now, instead of doing singular Fusions in my morning prayer/meditation time, I often intend to do Fusions on every single human on Earth. It is no additional effort and it can't possibly hurt. I like to think that in this way we are doing what the saints, gurus, masters, and mystics have been doing forever—radiating a high frequency resonant field to help lift human consciousness. Doing this puts us back in our power. We *can* change the world! Please let yourself be inspired to make Soul Body Fusion part of your ongoing spiritual practice and service to the world. My vision is that we consolidate the higher frequencies of our own divinity so powerfully in our body that we become a radiant light, spontaneously encouraging and igniting others to do the same—without effort or words.

The most difficult part of Soul Body Fusion is how easy it is. Our mind wants to make it complex, add steps, add rituals, add constraints, and ask questions. We talk about Soul Body Fusion being the "Easy Button." Let's get out of the limiting belief that the bigger the desired change, the harder the effort.

An Empty Chair

One idea of how to use Soul Body Fusion remotely was sent in by Anne from Norway. In this case Anne had an interesting visitor.

> *I often do Soul Body Fusion just by pretending I'm in a big room with anyone who wants to join me. Sometimes I visualize a chair in front of me. Often I visualize there are hundreds of people I can see. They don't always have faces, but they are there. I ask for anyone who wants to have a close-up SBF to sit down in the chair. I was doing this and I visualized a man come in and sit down. I knew him from my town and I knew that he had passed away two weeks before. So in my mind I said to him, "Why are you coming? You are dead!" He replied, "Oh, is that what happened?" So, I saw his light go up and away, and I guess he went to "heaven"!*

Animals

Once people do Soul Body Fusions on their family and friends, it only makes sense to try the process on pets and other animals. Anything with a physical component also has a spiritual, nonphysical existence. Whether you consider that animals have individualized souls or have group souls, it doesn't matter. What we see is that like humans, animals can benefit from the intentional blending of their material being with higher, finer, brighter frequencies of health and flow.

One story that comes to mind is from a Soul Body Fusion practitioner who worked remotely on her friend's sick horse. The horse's owner sat in the paddock with her ailing animal while the facilitator was on the phone in a different village, doing a ten-minute Fusion process for the horse. The owner was amazed that as soon as the ten minutes began, the horse immediately lay down in the grass. When the ten minutes were over, as if on cue, the horse stood up!

Using a photo, Grethe in Denmark worked remotely on a dog that was teetering on the edge of life and death, with a tetanus infection. She did Fusions four times on the dog during a couple of weeks. The animal made a remarkable recovery. In fact, when the owners brought the dog back to be examined, three veterinarians came to marvel at the dog's survival.

Tove in Norway was creative in her animal healing. Before New Year's Eve she decided that she could do something to help all the animals who get frightened from the loud sound of fireworks. So she announced on her Facebook page that she would do Fusions on everyone's animals for free that evening. All they had to do was post the animal's photo on her Facebook wall and agree to give her feedback on what happened. "I had dogs, cats, horses, even sheep," Tove told me laughingly. "*Everybody* said their pet was better!"

Those of us with animals are not surprised by how easily they pick this up and how well they respond to any changes in our energy. I did a Fusion on my neighbor Lori. She felt nothing during the process. "I feel nice," she said, more to be polite. However, her white terrier was spellbound. He stared at her the entire time, his tail wagging ferociously—sometimes letting out audible sighs. His behavior was so unusual that I experimented to see if he sensed the energies or was just concerned that I was touching his mistress. I sat with Lori in exactly the same position as before but without intending a Fusion. You got it: the dog settled down. It is my opinion that her beloved dog gave Lori the confirmation she needed that something did happen.

Objects and Life Situations

I never considered doing Fusions on inanimate objects or situations until White Eagle suggested it in a reading. Trent had been unable to sell his house, which had been on the market for several years. White Eagle suggested that Trent do a Fusion, bringing the spirit of the land more fully into the home and property. The suggestion made surprising sense to both of us. Trent tried it, even envisioning higher light coming in through an upstairs skylight. The Soul Body Fusion made a difference, as the house sold a few months later.

Upon hearing this example, Marie in Stockholm did Soul Body Fusion to find a new flat and to sell her existing home easily in a difficult market. She now uses it to create any flow in her life:

> *What I do is to set an intention for whatever I want with a certain situation and then I just think Soul Body Fusion. After that I leave the situation and allow it to create itself. I don't know if it is necessary to do SBF on situations or if it is enough to do Soul Body Fusion on myself, and when my soul and body are more fused, I automatically have the flow in my life. But with these results I don't dare stop!*

Thomas, a healer in Denmark, had this to say:

> *I do SBF to the world. We truly have a duty, a mission, to make a great difference for all humankind and for Earth. I also did SBF to our clinic for about five minutes. Within two hours three brand new clients came to us!*

Perhaps Soul Body Fusion isn't exactly the right name for what we're doing with homes and jobs. Whatever you call it, every situation can benefit by the focused intention of lifting it to a higher vibration for the best outcome for all. I encourage you to experiment on anything. Doing Soul Body Fusion teaches Soul Body Fusion. Remember: No Rules. Just try it!

Chapter 7

Healing and Healers

Miracles happen every day, and in medicine we like to attribute them to what we do or what others do around us. A lot of medicine is outside our control. We are wise to acknowledge miracles.
—Dr. G. Michael Lemole Jr.

Moving to Perfection

In our medical model, healing is usually focused on the elimination of symptoms in order to restore the patient back to their status quo. Only sometimes does healing go deep enough to transform the root cause of the disease. You might say that western, medically based healing moves a person from a negative (or below zero) state to a neutral (or zero) state. Soul Body Fusion is about expanding our potential at all levels, including material well-being.

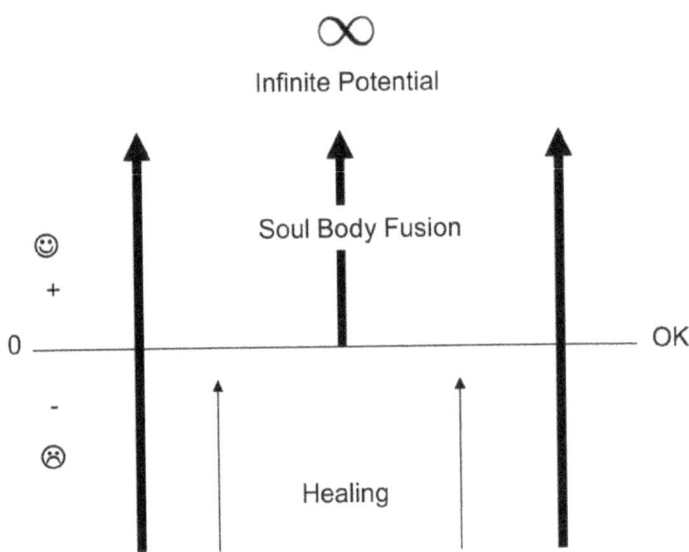

Healing vs. expanding infinite potential. Fig. 7.1.

Consider our diagram. SBF works above and below the zero line, bringing a person to a more and more positive state, not merely eliminating the negatives. In this way, SBF encompasses healing but is not strictly a healing tool. It is a tool for manifesting ever-expanding levels of potential. In our traditional healing paradigm we only jump into action when something is wrong and needs to be fixed. What about growing, expanding, and improving even when nothing is wrong? What about the opportunity of taking what's great about us and making it greater? Soul Body Fusion works on improving the positive side of the line, and in many cases healing the negative side—sickness and disease—happens as well. Although SBF has contributed to countless reports of extraordinary healing, it is much more.

In my work I have the opportunity to teach and assist thousands of people around the world in the areas of spiritual growth. As much as I am privileged to see the miracles of the human spirit, it breaks my heart to hear stories of illness, pain, and suffering. Until people have a level of comfort and wellness, it is nearly impossible for them to be able to focus on spiritual growth and the transformation of human consciousness. In response to this pain I committed deep in my soul to be a healer; not just a one-on one healer, but to somehow reach hundreds of thousands. As part of this quest I continued to practice my newly discovered process of Soul Body Fusion, and I looked for opportunities to be with some of the world's great healers.

John of God

In the fall of 2009 I traveled to Abadiânia, Brazil, to spend two weeks at the Casa de Dom Inácio, the healing center of the famed spiritualist healer John of God. The man known as *João* in his native Portuguese sits in trance for hours as hundreds of people, sometimes more than a thousand a day, line up to see him. Each person usually has less than fifteen seconds before him as he scribbles a symbol on a note or waves them into the next room, where his host of spirit guides work silently and invisibly. Many times he doesn't speak, or he says only a word or two. Over the decades there have been thousands of stories of seemingly miraculous healings. John of God humbly explains, "I do not heal. God is the one who heals."

The general process is that you write out specifically what you wish John of God's spirits to help you with. Your note is then translated into Portuguese, to be read to the illiterate healer. "I desire to be a healer of humankind," my note stated.

Instead of the usual nod and wave without a word, *João* spoke clearly the words that were then translated into English:

"I will help you." Tears of gratitude rolled down my face as I absorbed the power of those words. I was to be helped in my mission.

Over the next few days the question kept emerging: "*How will I be a healer of humankind?*" For a week I had no clue. Then a quote from Arthur Ashe, the tennis champion, came to mind: "To achieve greatness start where you are, use what you have, do what you can." Call me dense, but only then did I realize that I already had the means to be a healer… and beyond: I could use that simple process with which I was experimenting—Soul Body Fusion!

Many of you are drawn to Soul Body Fusion as a healing tool, so let's explore why a process in which no special skill is required can be effective. Soul Body Fusion creates what seems to be an electromagnetic change in the body. The word *magnetic* takes the whole thing out of the realm of *doing* into *being*. You can't *do* magnetic. Magnetism is a property of being. SBF isn't about doing healing as an activity. It is about being in the magnificent space of wholeness where health already exists. Soul Body Fusion focuses on your high state of being and your connection to your partner. It is about the space you hold with your focus and intention.

During the process you go to the highest space you can reach while still feeling grounded and stable. From that state you hold the knowledge that the other is fine, his or her soul is complete. Nothing is ever damaged when seen from the highest perspective. You hold your partner in an incredible field of love that sees the partner as perfect. I call this "God Consciousness." When God looks at you, God only sees perfection. It is that vision that drives the universe toward perfection. God doesn't manipulate.

God doesn't get involved in the details of your life, or any one's life. God's vision of perfection is so profound, it is so grounded in the truth, that holding this vision might be God's only job. We will all find perfection in our own sweet time, there is no doubt, because that is the only outcome possible. Soul Body Fusion helps us align our frame or field with the consciousness that God has always held. Ultimately there are no other possibilities.

The caduceus. Fig. 7.2

Soul Body Fusion in pairs is so powerful because it is a partnership. The intertwined twin serpents in the ancient caduceus symbol represent the fundamental principle that the healer and the one who appears to need healing are actually equal partners in a relationship that has the potential to go beyond the two to heal the collective matrix of humankind. I believe healing is therefore not only a one-on-one, singular event but the point at which negative patterns in the matrix that influence humanity can be accessed and reversed.

The Lamb and the Lion

Glenda Green tells a story about the nature of wholeness that continues to inspire me. Her wonderful book *Love Without End: Jesus Speaks* describes her extraordinary conversations with Jesus as she painted an exquisite portrait of him holding a lamb. In the 1990s she traveled to various churches, bringing along her gigantic oil painting of Jesus and sharing what she had learned from him. Before one presentation, tragedy struck. A falling floodlight crashed into the canvas, denting it and tearing a one-inch cut through the center. Glenda knew that even with professional restoration the painting could never be made whole; there would always be a dent. However, the next morning when she could finally bring herself to inspect the damage, she was shocked to see that the injury was gone! In its place, "there was **only perfection**; no dent, no cut, no loss of paint.... Not so much as a fiber was torn."[10] Glenda wrote: "There exists an expanded consciousness that retained a perception of the painting's whole-ness despite the assault! It seems as though my normal perceptions of reality, which extend horizontally, had been intersected by a vertical insertion of a higher truth and power." She raised the question: "Could it be that nothing but wholeness ever does prevail once we are willing to perceive it?"[11]

My belief is that it is an old paradigm to heal what is broken. Our greater opportunity is to focus on a state of consciousness or wholeness where it was never broken in the first place—moving beyond cause and effect to the God essence of perfection.

It's Not About You

I invite us all to expand beyond the medical mind set in which a diagnosis turns a person into a patient, the patient is placed on a treatment conveyer belt and from then on all personal power is steadily given over to the experts, the doctors, the drugs, the procedures. True and permanent healing must come from your own power, which of course includes the power of your higher self. The simplicity of Soul Body Fusion honors this. The power for healing and transcendence is always yours. When you work with a partner in the Fusion, you are equals—twin serpents on the caduceus staff. In the beginning it may look as if the experienced one is giving a Fusion to another, but in reality you are holding the other in a loving space and your resonance is showing the way. In a flash his/her higher spirit picks up the vibrational invitation and they're off— healing, tingling, opening up. It is a partnership that is more appropriately called healer/healer.

Let's look at the future of healing from a higher dimensional point of view. This explanation is from my spirit guide Mark in response to the question "Why are so many healers sick or unemployed?"

> *I'm going to break some paradigms. I'm going to answer from a sixth and seventh-dimensional perspective. This answer may not make much sense in the strictly third-dimensional level. Some rules for the 3D world are not the same rules as in the higher-dimensional realms. Much as in physics, Newtonian physics works most of the time, except with subatomic particles. They don't listen to Newton. They have different rules. While people believe in healing, they believe in separation; that one person is broken and another has the ability to fix them.*

There are two myths here. One is that someone can be broken. That is false in the higher dimensions. The other myth is that someone else can do something about it. So healing is appropriate in the 3D world. But as you move into the higher dimensions, then being a healer and seeing people as in need of healing will continue to create sickness. It will create it in the healer and the healed. Again, this can make you upset, but I am giving answers that are true in the higher worlds, the realms to which you aspire. In your world, as it is structured now, healing—because it is accepted by people—is effective. But as healers begin moving more of their selves to the higher dimensions, then being a healer is going to backfire. In the higher worlds the idea of healing someone else causes separation, and it could cause sickness. When you are more comfortable in the higher dimensions, this answer will make more sense.

Real, soul-sourced healing isn't about your skill—it's about the other. I learned this in the 1990s when I, as a new Reiki Master, was teaching Reiki II for the first time. I've always been a diligent student—studying, memorizing, practicing; yes, and worrying if I was good enough. So I approached my Reiki lessons the same way. If my own, rather traditional Reiki Master suggested that I should hold my breath during the complex initiation process, then I held my breath. When he suggested that I could create an important energy flow in my body by putting the tip of my tongue behind my teeth and simultaneously contracting the perineum (the region between the anus and the genitals), I held my breath, kept my tongue locked behind my teeth, and contracted my entire pelvic region since I had no idea how to isolate my perineum. While I was doing all this, I was supposed to draw a series of complicated Reiki symbols over the head, back, and hands of the initiate. Simultaneously I was to connect them with the higher flows of the Reiki energies.

Because I can't hold my breath very long, I raced through the complicated symbols—visualizing several wrong. In my haste I completely forgot to feel the flow of energy and connect to it. My tongue was behind my teeth in a most unnatural way; my lower body was cramped from trying to contract my perineum; and I was nearly blue from holding my breath during my first student's initiation… and I still had nine more students to go! Gasping for breath, feeling guilty that I hadn't done a good job, I got the clear insight that this whole thing had become about *me*… about *me* doing a good job, doing what I had been told. I was so much in my head that the spiritual, heart process of connection was lost. It was no longer about them and the natural flow of divine energies. I made a new decision that changed how I look at my role as a healer from that moment on. I focused on the feel of the Reiki energies, on taking my time with the symbols. I stopped holding my breath, holding my tongue, and tightening my darned perineum. I'm sure the next nine students actually felt the shift. I was there to serve them, not to do it right.

In another humorous incident about a decade later, I was reminded again that it's not about me. At the time my healing abilities were growing significantly as my spiritual work accelerated, so I thought it would be nice to offer free remote healing for the month of May. I assumed that it would stretch and sharpen my skills and hopefully help people I wouldn't otherwise reach. I asked my office assistant Dave to send an email out only to our inner group of one hundred or so students, offering free healing for a month. They were to email me their name, age, physical location, and illness or problem. My plan was to write down all their details and work on each person individually every morning and night. The emailed requests for help came in. Then they *poured* in. From all over the world hundreds and hundreds of detailed requests flooded my electronic in-basket! I didn't know these people! Many were from countries I had never visited. What happened here? Dave sheepishly admitted that he had misunderstood my request to offer free healing to a small segment of my students. Instead he sent the offer to our entire database, and many sent it to their databases as well!

With so many heartfelt requests for healing, I couldn't do them one at a time as I had planned. I printed out pages and pages of names and illnesses. My intention was to meditate and to visualize gathering them together into an ethereal healing temple in order to work on them en masse. Once I got myself into a high and settled space, I planned to read the lists to begin the healing. But an amazing vision appeared in my mind's eye. The hundreds of people *weren't waiting for me* to do healing on them! They were milling about, connecting, touching, talking, and healing each other! A person with good legs and a bad liver was being healed by a person with bad legs and a good liver. My jaw dropped. I wasn't needed! Perhaps my role was to invite them, through my intention, to a high vibrational space where healing naturally happens. I laughed a long time and have never taken my healing powers seriously again. It isn't about me and it isn't about you. Isn't that a huge relief?

Perhaps Tove in Norway said it best: The hardest part is to get people to know they can do this. For the last two years all my healing is just intent. I have full confidence this works. I am. I don't give. No one can fix anything in you. You must do it yourself.

Healing Stories

Here are various stories of healing submitted from around the world. Reading them can give you an idea of the immense possibilities from SBF.

Øyvind, Norway

> *Three years ago I was diagnosed with type-2 diabetes and took medication three times a day. I met Tove, who was giving SBF on Facebook. I had no faith in energy healing. But when she gave me SBF a few times, I felt pins and needles in my hands and head and it felt good. It felt like the energy in my body grew each time. After the first Fusion, I was gradually able scale back on my diabetes drugs. I even took the class and we all gave Fusions to each other. For the last twelve days I have not taken any medicine. I have not made any changes in my diet or exercise. My blood sugar is stable, even without medication. I believe SBF has fixed my body so it produces insulin normally again. This is huge evidence that SBF works. I was just now at the doctor's and he confirmed that I no longer have diabetes! I cannot find another explanation for this except Soul Body Fusion.*

Anne, Norway

> *A skeptical friend, who had been treated medically for depression, came to see me because he was about to enter a new period of depression. When he came for the second Fusion he told me, "There's something happening and I don't understand what." At his third session he admitted that the Fusion worked in the same way*

> as his medicine works—he was notable to hold onto his negative thinking and he didn't go into the negative spiral. This time he managed without medical treatment. The effects of SBF are still working, and eight months have passed.

Gurli, Denmark

> I did a fusion on a very depressed man. He only let me do it for thirty seconds before he told me, "I can't do this." And he went out for a smoke. When he came back, there were stars in his eyes. He told me, "Something happened. I am happier." Later he began to open up the psychic and spiritual gifts that were closed down before.

Anna, Finland

Anna is a medical doctor who specializes in acupuncture. She is also a Soul Body Fusion Certified Teacher.

> I do a lot of Fusions on menopausal women, and they aren't very pleased afterward, because most of them started menstruating again! Actually they feel younger, more relaxed, peaceful, and with more life flowing inside them... they are happier!

> The most important experiences have been with sexually abused women. One patient told me she had never been in her body; she "lives on the roof." I could sense something very painful was behind all her symptoms, as she had had psychotic episodes and many physical issues. So I began doing SBF while she was processing the acupuncture. As a result, her life changed tremendously. She remains in her body. She started dating,

where in the past she'd had no relationships. She comes and asks for "all those things you do for me again."

Aina, Norway

A drug addict. After I gave him SBF four times, he became visibly calm and happy, and this state lasted several days. His dyslexia is better. Instead of going out into space and trying to "leave," he is more stable. *A bipolar person* had tremendous results at once. She has halved the dose of medication and is very functional. She has become more stable and is also able to face her issues. She sleeps better and is not afraid of her fears. She is letting go of her anxiety and old belief systems. She tells me that she loves to live and wants more Soul Body Fusion. *A girl with autistic behavior* came in very unstable and nervous. During the Fusion she fell asleep on the table. After the Fusion she became very calm and was able to receive. That is rare. Her mother told me that she was "here" for many days after the first session. She felt safer in her daily life.

My experience is that my clients see themselves more clearly, able to view their own situation without fear. They are more able to assist in their treatments. Soul Body Fusion showed me that it is possible to do something quickly and effortlessly. I call it the "Easy Button."

Birgit, Germany

I did an SBF on my son, who is twelve years old and suffers from a lot of fears. He clings to us and is afraid to be in another room alone. His bed had to be in *our bedroom. When I sat down with him to do the SBF and touched his fingers, he felt uncomfortable and could not sit still. He said, "Mommy, when will it end? Can you stop it?" My mind was asking, "What am I doing to my child?" But my soul told me to just stay connected. So I did. He was nearly crying. Nothing much happened during that first week.*

When we did the second session, he calmly sat in front of me like he was nailed to the floor. He said that he could sit forever in this position—grounded in his legs and his feet. This time the flow was so easy he didn't want me to stop. The first time, it felt like something was stuck, but the second and third times were completely different! He is re ally changing now! When he goes into a room, he doesn't even realize that the light isn't on. He's not afraid of the dark. He can sleep in his own room now! It is wonderful to be able to do this!

Kjell, Norway

I have been a healer for about five years and use a lot of different techniques. But learning Soul Body Fusion really changed my understanding of what healing can do if we allow ourselves to open up for the possibilities of the universe to work. It is incredible that with so little effort the results can be so great.

I have seen similar results with many of my clients. They describe a bubbling in the blood, and their bodies start to relax all over. Slowly their mind relaxes too. The effect on many is that their wrinkles start to be reduced, since they no longer have their brains filled with so much thinking. Not a bad effect!

I've also seen weight loss. A friend, lost five kilos after she suddenly started to breathe more deeply after two healings of Soul Body Fusion. She had tried every trick in the book for many years unsuccessfully until she tried this technique.

No promises here! But being integrated allows us to really listen to our body rather than numb it with food. Also, when toxicity gets released with the Fusion, it enables the body to shed protective fat cells.

The strongest effect I've seen was on a twelve year-old girl. Her mother came for a consultation and brought her along. The mother told me that her daughter hadn't laughed or smiled for over a year, not since she saw her father threatening her mother. I asked if I could try Soul Body Fusion on her daughter. During this, the girl suddenly started to cry, and her body began to shake a lot. At the end of the session she started to laugh and her mother reported that she was happy for a long time afterwards. The mother commented that her daughter had not shown any feelings for a year, until she suddenly reacted during the Soul Body Fusion session.

Birgitte, Denmark

My neighbor slipped on some ice the other day, hurting herself badly. At the hospital they took some X-rays of her leg/knee and found a fracture. They wanted her to have a CT scan the following day before they did an operation.

She was in great pain and asked me for help. I gave her SBF three times. At one point I "felt" the fracture, but I just let the energy work. Remember—I didn't do anything. When she had the scan the next day, they could not find any fracture and she didn't need an operation. She can walk around and is not in a lot of pain. She has never experienced things getting better so fast. I am convinced that Soul Body Fusion has done the healing. I clearly felt the fracture and it is not there anymore.

Fusions with Cancer Patients

Yvana from Switzerland, a Soul Body Fusion Certified Teacher, shares her inspiring experiences with cancer patients and patients with mental illnesses. First, for some context, we'll begin with a little information about Yvana and how she came to interact with so many people dealing with cancer.

I never thought of myself as a healer. I was born very sensitive, into a reality that I perceived as challenging. Being sexually abused as a baby caused a major disconnection from my body that lasted until I discovered Soul Body Fusion two years ago (I'm forty-six now). My gratefulness for this simple and effective tool is beyond words! SBF allowed me to feel safe in my body for the first time. The absence of that during most of my life made me want to escape reality. Which I did by diving into all kinds of addictions, like excessive reading, chocolate, drugs, TV, video gaming, and partying.

I had jobs at banks and in the Swiss government until I had a sudden physical breakdown followed by almost unbearable pain—without doctors being able to find anything wrong. That was a wake up call from my body, to bring it into my consciousness; telling me it was time to end the escaping and start living in it. I couldn't understand the signs, until a couple of months later I was diagnosed with aggressive breast cancer. That's when the rest of my being experienced a breakdown too, falling into a deep depression, so deep I was not able to deal with my disease or the outside world at all. It was an intense time of self-contemplation and letting go of all the musts, to do's, and many of my fears. Still, the relationship with my body was rather fragile. I didn't fully trust in it, expecting it to break down again any minute.

At that point I watched Jonette doing a group Soul Body Fusion over the internet. I had never felt anything like it before! Not only did I feel absolutely connected with my body in a loving, caring way, but also I was receiving all those feelings I'd never had, like safety, completeness, and peace! This moved me right out of the "stucknesss" and I started to deal with my disease, visiting doctors again for the first time in years, getting all the necessary checkups. The results were frustrating: three different doctors predicted a survival chance of only 62 percent, and that only if my breast was removed immediately, followed by years of intense therapy with chemo, radiation, and anti-hormones. Meanwhile, Jonette announced her first Soul Body Fusion workshop in Germany. I clearly knew this was for me! Postponing the surgery, I participated in the workshop, which turned out to be life-changing! After we practiced Soul Body Fusion with each other for about two hours, I felt completely healed! I connected to a love so huge, unconditional, and all surpassing—pure bliss! I began to do Soul Body Fusion on every occasion with anyone open to it, starting with the taxi driver from the workshop. This technique really seems to be the easiest way to integrate all of oneself.

At each session, the feeling of being healed returned and I basked in it. I was able to face my fears and go right through them. A couple of months later I felt the time was right for the surgery. Here is where my personal miracle started: Everything went so well, like a surreal dream! I felt accompanied by my soul throughout, incredibly safe and loved. The doctors were able to easily remove the tumor without having to remove my breast! They mentioned that they've never seen a four-year-old, 380-gram tumor without any metastases elsewhere in the body! My tests were so good I didn't need chemotherapy or radiation. I believe that all my body needs is for me to do SBF on myself on a regular basis, because of this complete, conscious presence! I was able to raise my awareness to such a degree that now I know what caused me to create that cancer in myself.

The miracle continued: After the easy surgery, my parents unexpectedly asked me to stay at their house for nurturing until I went to a healing center. Now that the manifestation of my disconnection with my body had been removed, the return to the origin of this disconnection was one grand healing trip! Everything appeared fresh and new—cleared of the old. Even my childhood room had lost its shadow. In that moment I felt it so clearly: the abuse is healed! The feelings were indescribably beautiful. Like one big happy celebration. My parents treated me like a queen, with their love and care. They noticed the free flow as well, and ever since then they always want me to visit to experience this unique, wonderful feeling.

After this visit, I moved for four weeks into an anthroposophical healing center in Switzerland, founded by Rudolf Steiner, which specializes in cancer. Humans are treated holistically there. I enjoyed the treatments, the healthy food, and the wonderful garden. My magical story with Soul Body Fusion was embraced with wide-open arms and spread quickly. Soon I was approached by interested persons who wanted to try it out. That's when my wonderful journey started, where I was able to witness firsthand the huge impact it can have on cancer patients! From the second week until my stay ended, I was busy doing up to five Fusions per day. Which served me equally: By the time I left, doctors confirmed that I would not need any additional therapies (such as chemo, radiation, and anti-hormones) and that I am totally free of cancer! So Soul Body Fusion not only prevented me from undergoing years of exhausting therapies but also helped save my left breast—and my life.

Here are Yvana's accounts of giving Soul Body Fusion to three seriously ill cancer patients. The descriptions of the patients and their diagnoses are based on the information these patients gave Yvana directly.

"D," forty-seven years old, had a melanoma (cancer cells) in her left eye and metastases in the entire body.

Doctors said there was barely any chance of curing her except by chemotherapy.

While facilitating the SBF, I experienced beautiful, intense feelings.

The next morning "D" had rising memories of childhood sexual abuse. In the following weeks she processed related emotions intensely. After the third session, "D" acquired a wonderful understanding of how this childhood event connected to her self-destroying patterns: She started to see again. This had a big impact on her health: Her test results improved significantly; she felt better each day, very energized. Chemotherapy was not even a subject anymore. Today, seven months later, she has resolved the entire childhood problem with her family and feels great, emotionally and physically. She travels the world, experiencing beautiful spiritual encounters, and enjoys life to the fullest. The metastases in the body have completely disappeared without chemotherapy.

A year after the SBF, although she still has a small melanoma in the eye, it no longer affects her eyesight or her health.

Did you notice that when the patient began to *see* her childhood patterns, the cancer that started in her eye, diminished? For many people it is the clarity about the cause of their illness that allows them to release it and heal.

"E," forty-four years old, *had breast cancer— her body traumatized by the loss of her right breast and eight months of chemotherapy. She was totally disconnected* *from the right side of her body, with intense pain from the removal of over forty lymph nodes; she could not sit in the same position longer than a few minutes because of the pain; she had difficulty sleeping through the night because of the anti-hormones. She felt disillusioned regarding treatments, doctors, and humanity in general; grumpy, distanced, and a loner.*

While doing the Fusion on her, I felt incredible warmth, like never before. My hands were dripping. A deep love filled the space.

"E" immediately connected with her right side, as feeling returned to it for the first time since the operation. With her body vibrating, especially the right, all her pain left in that moment! She sat for more than half an hour perfectly still, enjoying the beautiful, intense feelings. Next day she intuitively stopped taking anti-hormones and started making choices for herself, facing her anger and sadness, transforming it, and learning how to cry—something she hadn't been able to do her whole life. She's lightening up, feeling better every day, telling jokes, socializing. The pain has diminished steadily to a bearable minimum. Only three months after SBF, tests showed such improvement it allowed her to have her right breast reconstructed completely, without further chemotherapy. Today, another four months later, she feels great, continuing to choose the best options for herself and allowing necessary changes to happen, like leaving an unhealthy relationship behind, moving into a cozy apartment of her own, and focusing on joyful activities.

"G," fifty-four years old, *had cancer in every part of her body, including the head, and was very weakened by years of chemotherapy and pain; she could barely walk without help and hadn't enough energy even to talk. Doctors said she was incurable and had a life expectancy of three months at most.*

We held the SBF session in the garden, barefooted. From the beginning, I felt as if ants were crawling over my face, and I had a very strong urge to scratch. I then realized that this wasn't mine and just focused on breathing my soul into my body." Then "G" said: "It literally felt as if death was crawling out of my body into your hands! I was supported by Earth, with which I was deeply connected. Now I feel free and complete."

The next day "G" was walking about by herself, energized—looking ten years younger and very present. She entertained a table of seven people, laughing and enjoying that moment free of pain. Today, seven months later, "G" is still living. Some of the pain is back and she is facing physical and emotional challenges, but her tests improve after every SBF session, and doctors say she absolutely should continue whatever she does, for it is the reason she is still alive—which is a miracle.

These are the three most remarkable examples I witnessed of the powerful impact that Soul Body Fusion can have on people with cancer. Overall, I did SBF with over thirty cancer patients. The most common experience afterwards was a significant reduction in pain and an improvement in test results—and quality of life. Emotionally, patients experienced loving, peaceful, warm feelings and a sense of being complete like never before. After SBF about 75 percent quit conventional treatments, such as chemotherapy, radiation, and anti hormones—and they are living a richer, healthier life today, making time for joy.

Yvana's Examples of SBF for Mental Illness

The connection to the institution with mentally disabled people took place in the cancer center. A stranger asked me what technique I was using, and I answered "Soul Body Fusion." Then I speculated about a possible evaluation of the effect of SBF on people with mental disorders and whether medications could be reduced. To my great surprise, she was a director for a mental institution and was always in search of new treatment options! I realized that my passionate speech about Soul Body Fusion was synchronistic.

Before going into her experiences with people with mental imbalances, Yvana prefaced the account by saying that unfortunately she never received a professional perspective on her results and she was not able to follow up on the patients with whom she worked. Her account continues below.

Curious about how Soul Body Fusion would affect mental handicaps, I was guided to a patient seated alone. I started talking with him. Soon he asked what I was doing. I said, "Soul Body Fusion."

He lightened up visibly and introduced me to his buddies, yelling, "She does Soul Body Fusion, people, Soul

Body Fusion!" Five patients began bombarding me with questions. I set the intent to do SBF with all of them right in that moment, while talking. After a bit there was a significant opening up in three in our little group. They shared:

"F," **forty-five years old** (unknown mental diagnosis), had a criminal record and severe drug past. Has taken methadone for ten years and just had his daily dose. Hence, he drifted away most of the time. Setting the SBF intent brought him into the present quickly; remarkable also were his eyes: they radiated an accepting, embracing love, when before they looked rushed and wild. His energy softened, and he appeared at total ease with himself. He said he felt special in that moment and very safe—a feeling he'd forgotten a long time ago.

"P," **thirty-two years old,** had been diagnosed with schizophrenia. She was traumatized by a childhood of violence and sexual abuse and needs psychotic medication. She asked the most questions. As she had a sensitive nature, I felt her communicating on many different levels. The most beautiful thing she said was how she felt that some of her missing parts were coming back again and how inspired she was by the idea that SBF could help her get whole again!

"W," **thirty-seven years old,** had been diagnosed with paranoia. He was afraid of others and had an alcohol problem. Very sensitive, he felt most safe when behind his four walls with the door locked, playing video games; he needed psychotic medication.

His transformation after SBF was the most significant: he turned from a cynic, a locked-in, rejecting person with huge walls, into a friendly, loving man who openly talked about his aspirations. After he told his life story, I asked him if this felt challenging for him, especially with his background.

Enthusiastically he replied, "Noooo, not in this moment!"

In this one magical moment after Soul Body Fusion these three wonderful people felt healed and clear! It would be interesting to hear whether that state lasted and whether there were any remarkable changes in their behavior. Nevertheless, already these results are amazing and mark the infinite potentials of Soul Body Fusion. I wouldn't want to miss a second of this experience, which continues to be beautiful and special.

There is nothing I love more than exploring the infinite potentials of Soul Body Fusion. What a wonderful tool! May it touch many more lives and help them realize what beautiful and complete beings we all are!!! I'm looking forward to experiencing and discovering many more potentials of SBF—for this is truly joyful!

We are all so grateful for the incredible work Yvana has done as part of her own healing and expanding journey of service. And thanks, Yvanna, for taking such good notes! They are a huge contribution to the growth of Soul Body Fusion!

PART III

Going Deeper

I invite humans to give up the vision of what you think you want so the vision of possibilities may be unlimited, to hold in your hearts the reality of a discontinuous transfiguration. This is a time of grail and goddess.

-Ashtatara

Chapter 8

Science and the Soul

The most beautiful and profound emotion we can experience is the sensation of the mystical. It is the power of all true science.

-Albert Einstein

Testing SBF on the "Map of Consciousness" Scale

You've read the stories—some people reporting increases in health, wholeness, happiness, and spiritual gifts following Soul Body Fusion. I became curious to learn if there is something we can actually measure, beyond a person's direct experience of the Fusion process. I understand that subtle energy shifts are notoriously difficult to document. With the soul, we don't even know if we are dealing with actual energy at all, even in its more subtle forms. What we call the soul could be a field beyond the spectrum of energy as we know it.

Our first experiment was a simple *before*-and-*after* Soul Body Fusion test with a group of eight people who had never experienced SBF previously. We used applied kinesiology, sometimes called muscle testing, to calibrate people's consciousness levels according to the Map of Consciousness scale developed by Sir David R. Hawkins, MD, PhD, Director of the Institute for Advanced Spiritual Research, and explained in his book *Power vs. Force*. Underlying the practice of kinesiology is the premise that our body is connected to higher wisdom. We can find answers—true/false, yes/no—if we disconnect our rational brain and directly ask questions or make statements of our body, testing the answer by the strength of our muscle response. You might say that true wisdom is a no-brainer! In the muscle testing used by Dr. Hawkins and many professional kinesiologists, the subjects will hold out their arm and focus on keeping it strong while the tester makes a statement and meanwhile places downward pressure, gently but firmly, on the upraised arm. A "yes," or strong result, is indicated if the subject can easily resist the pressure, maintaining the strength of his or her arm. In a weak, or "no," response the subject is unable to resist the pressure and the arm sags or falls.

Through research, experimentation, and extensive corroboration using kinesiology, Dr. Hawkins created a logarithmic scale from 1 to 1000 to measure human consciousness: 1 is the value for merely being alive, while 1000 indicates a totally advanced state of enlightenment. On this scale, 200 is the critical level. It is the dividing line between force (below 200) and power (above 200). Therefore, anything that calibrates below 200 will test as weak, everything at or above 200 will test as strong. Hawkins describes force as needy and constantly consuming; it polarizes rather than unifies. It is a movement *against* something. In contrast, power arises from meaning and is life enhancing. Power is still and is complete unto itself. Power gives forth, supplies, and supports. Therefore, power is associated with positive feelings, love, and compassion.

Moving up the scale on the Map of Consciousness, Dr. Hawkins found that love calibrates at 500. People who calibrate above 500 have the happiness of others as an essential motivator. "The high 500s are characterized by interest in spiritual awareness for both oneself and others, and by the 600s, the good of mankind and the search for enlightenment are the primary goals." In other words, 600 represents the apex of ordinary consciousness. Hawkins continues, "From 700 to 1000, life is dedicated to the salvation of all of humanity."[12] It is interesting that in 1995 Hawkins used this scale to look at the overall evolution of consciousness. "The collective consciousness of consciousness of mankind remained at 190 for many centuries and, curiously, only jumped to its current level of 207 within the last decade."[13] I would add my presumption that our human consciousness has continued to increase above 207 since Dr. Hawkins first published his results in 1995. This would account in part for the very high consciousness numbers we found in our testing of eight people.

We wanted to run an experiment in which we first tested subjects' consciousness on the Hawkins scale of 1 to 1000 and then answered the question "What difference does Soul Body Fusion make to that score?" We hired Neil Habgood, Advanced Core Health Facilitator (www.RealHealthinc.org), a practitioner trained in the clinical application of comprehensive kinesiology. He himself had never experienced Soul Body Fusion. Neil performed a baseline muscle test to find each person's starting position relative to the Hawkins Map of Consciousness before they received a standard two-phase, twenty-minute SBF session. Following the Fusion, Neil retested each of the eight participants. Our test group consisted of six women and two men, ranging in ages between twenty-five and eighty-three. Here are the results:

Person	Before	After	Net Change
A	357	360	+3
B	735	742	+7
C	255	264	+9
D	316	319	+3
E	414	421	+7
F	852	861	+9
G	905	915	+10
H	435	456	+21
Mean	534	542	+9

Even though the sample was small, it is statistically significant that in *every instance* the volunteers experienced an increase in consciousness after a single Soul Body Fusion session. Here are the written comments from Neil Habgood:

> *As a kinesiologist performing thousands of measurements per year, it is rare to discover a process that creates a true, **measurable** shift in an individual's level of consciousness. After performing before-and-after measurements with the eight individuals who experienced Jonette's process, I was blown away by the results. Clearly, the Soul Body Fusion method has proven to provide each participant with a reliable, specific process to achieve an **instantaneous** increase in one's overall level of consciousness. To put these results in perspective, according to Dr. David Hawkins, the average individual will increase his/her consciousness level three to*

*five points in a lifetime. The participants of Jonette's Soul Body Fusion method experienced increases in consciousness ranging from three points to twenty-one points over a **twenty-minute time period**. Amazing!*

Just to be sure that such changes were the result of the SBF and not random, over the next week Neil did similar before-and-after muscle tests with eight of his clients. He allowed twenty minutes between the tests but otherwise performed no intervention. None of the eight showed so much as a single point change in their calibration on the scale!

The results we got with kinesiology regarding Soul Body Fusion are indicative of the same sort of immediate shifts people are reporting when they experience a Fusion. Dr. Hawkins himself stated: "In every studied case of recovery from hopeless and untreatable disease, there has been this major shift in consciousness."[14] To me it makes sense that merging more completely with your soul will move you upward in your consciousness growth.

Try It Yourself

I use arm muscle testing to demonstrate the power of attitude when I teach Enlightened Leadership courses to corporate clients. I ask for a volunteer to come in front of the class and say his name out loud, "My name is Paul," for instance. At the same time I put slight downward pressure on his raised arm while Paul tries to keep his arm strong. With ease Paul can resist my pushing. Then I ask him to tell the class, "My name is Shirley." You can guess the outcome. His arm is weak in the face of the incorrect statement. Now that a baseline is established and the audience can clearly see the difference between a strong and weak response, I have him turn his back and close his eyes. I then show the audience a thumbs up or a thumbs down sign, instructing them to silently have a positive attitude toward Paul—sending good vibes—on a thumbs up, and a negative attitude on a thumbs down. We do four or five random attitude shifts toward Paul, who is unaware of what thoughts we are holding. In every case so far, when the group holds negative thoughts toward the person the arm test is weak. Conversely, the arm is strong and unyielding when the class holds a positive attitude toward the volunteer.

The class is amazed at the influence their thoughts have on their colleague. The more verbal skeptics remark, "How can that be?" Or, "I don't believe it." At that point I get them out of their chairs in pairs to muscle test each other, after which the disbelievers are silenced. The point we make in organizations is that we know—our body knows—when an environment is positive, supportive, and safe, and we respond with strength: good decisions, more efficiency, and fewer mistakes. When we pick up negativity, intolerance, or judgment, our body is weak, resulting in slower work, more mistakes, and weaker overall performance. The body's changes between strong and weak are real, consistent, and demonstrable. However, don't let this lead you to think that your personal power is at the mercy of the environment and other people. It isn't. If you are positive, grounded and happy, your arm will be strong no matter how much negativity surrounds you.

Don't believe it? Here is an experiment you can try with a friend. First, establish a baseline by making a true statement out loud while your friend pushes down—not too hard, on your raised arm. Now say a lie while your partner muscle tests. This gives you the feeling of your positive and negative response. Now, say "Yes" out loud and test the arm. Say "No," and check your strength. What happens? Experiment another way. In this instance put yourself in a bad mood—focusing on all you have to do, or something that upsets you. Have your partner test your arm. Or, put yourself in a happy frame of mind and test again. Change it up without telling your partner what you are thinking. Your partner should be able to determine where your focus is, based on your arm strength. About 95 percent of the time your arm clearly indicates your positive or negative state of mind!

Take this discussion to the next level. Rather than just holding positive thoughts, imagine the actual physical advantages to your life when you use your focus to merge fully with your soul or higher self.

While we're discussing kinesiology, another demonstration I sometimes do with audiences shows the physical cost of our unconscious entrainment with the chaos around us. Let's use Paul again. As he stands in front of the group I go around messing things up on the stage. I throw markers on the floor, kick off my shoes haphazardly, and turn a chair upside down—in short, creating chaos. However, I say nothing. Without any instruction except "Please raise your arm and resist while I muscle test you again," Paul tries to withstand my pressure. What happens? Paul's arm is weak, even if I do the test several times. Why? As Paul observed my disordering actions his psyche unconsciously attuned or entrained to the surrounding field of chaos, causing his body to show weakness. If I had reminded Paul to focus on his core power, or the presence of his soul, no matter what clutter was around him, his arm would test strong. The point here is that when you are unconscious of your attention and not centered positively in yourself, you can easily be negatively impacted by the attendant chaos. Having your soul fully present in your life will be continuous insurance against being thrown so quickly off track.

The next time you do a Soul Body Fusion in person, first muscle test your partner's arm, stating: "On the Map of Consciousness scale from 1 to 1000, (name of the person)'s current consciousness level is _____?" Then start eliminating whole ranges of numbers. You might begin by asking: "…is above 200? Is above 300? Is above 400?" and so on until you find the *before* SBF value. Do the Fusion session, then conduct the same test to see if and by how much the Fusion had an impact on the Map of Consciousness score.

Testing Using Biofeedback

In this next experiment with Soul Body Fusion we were looking for any physiological changes as measured by three standard biofeedback indicators, in a simple before-and-after test. Our researcher, Liana Mattulich, MD, BCD, BCN, is a vivacious woman in her seventies. She is a doctor in both western and oriental medicine, an internationally recognized expert in the field of biofeedback and consciousness, and author of *Journey to Awareness and Beyond: with Modern Technology and Ancient Wisdom*. She explained, "Subtle energy is hard to quantify with science. Tiny changes in the physiology show us the actions of different subtle energies."

We brought in eight volunteers who had never had Soul Body Fusion before. Dr. Mattulich put heat sensors on their fingers to test temperature; then added a sensor to the palm of their hand to monitor electro-dermal response (this indicates the flow of thoughts and emotions). Finally she taped a probe to the top of each volunteer's head to measure the amplitude and frequency of dominant brain waves. All this was hooked up to a special biofeedback computer. She was especially interested in the difference in temperatures between a person's right and left hands. "We don't have good mind/body communication," she told me. "Most people don't have any idea which hand is warmer, and if they guess, they usually get it wrong." I sat wondering how out of balance we've become, and how we are so dissociated with ourselves that we don't even notice that we are out of balance.

The premise behind biofeedback is the innate wisdom of our body to follow our instructions and intention. Do you notice that this is the same mechanism at work when we invoke our soul in a Fusion? In the case of the thermal sensors on the fingers, the computer monitor shows us the temperature of each hand as a separate line on a graph. When the researcher tells us to warm up both hands to the same temperature, our body knows what to do. Our eyes watch the lines on the computer screen as, hopefully, the gap between our hand temperatures shrinks and they warm. If, for instance, both hands begin to get colder, we would notice the shift on the screen and our mind would tell our body, "Oops, whatever you're doing is making my hands cold, not warm. Do something else." In this case we are assisted by a computer to feed back data to our body so it can make the adjustments it knows how to make. However, computer technology isn't required. According to Dr. Mattulich, "Bodies can make efficient physical adjustments by applying techniques and practices used in ancient wisdom schools. What Soul Body Fusion does is just that; it is a wisdom technique that changes the possibilities of the psychophysiology."

Throughout our research day, Dr. Mattulich hooked our volunteers up to the computer, first for a baseline test. Then a Soul Body Fusion practitioner did a Fusion on each of them. This was followed by post-Fusion biofeedback sessions. Five of the eight had moderate improvements in their metrics. These ranged from warmer, more balanced hands to calmer, more centered brain wave patterns; to indicators of am ore connected mind and body.

In the before-and-after tests, three people had particularly significant shifts. One young woman, Terri (not her real name), who had recently left her husband and moved alone to Colorado, showed a disturbing pattern before the Fusion. Her emotional response line was totally flat and lay on the bottom of the graph—showing virtually no activity. Her hands were cold, her muscles tense. The biofeedback indicated that her emotions were repressed, controlled, contracted. "In that state she can receive no help," Dr. Mattulich explained to me later as we reviewed the graphs.

Terri wrote her experience of the Soul Body Fusion process: "My mind felt incredibly focused, asking to feel something from my soul, but I felt no emotion. My body became very light and I lost my physical orientation. I felt like I was floating and slightly buzzing. I thought about how different my life would be if I could bring my soul into my body."

After the Fusion, the graphs showed her hands warmer. Based on the changes in her dermal response and brain waves, Dr. Mattulich commented to me, "She is now open to receive. Now someone can work with her; before, she was shutting out everything."

Donna, an attractive woman in her early seventies, had a dramatic change in the frequency of her dominant brain waves after the Fusion. She was easily able to maintain this higher, healthy pattern for more than three minutes. "If someone can hold a harmonious pattern in the brain for three minutes, the body has a mechanism to deposit a nuclear protein, thus creating a new pathway. Now the new, improved pathway is anchored and stored in the brain." Dr. Mattulich explained.

The last young woman we saw that day, Claudia, had a

20-percent increase in the efficiency of her brain after the Fusion. The biofeedback graphs indicated that she was more centered, consistent, and secure. However, these scientifically measurable changes were nothing compared to the healing Claudia received in her Soul Body Fusion. Reina and Trent, both SBF Certified Teachers, partnered together to do the process with Claudia. Here are Reina's words:

Claudia is sensitive and could feel what was going on. She had many sensations and broke down and cried for a time. I had the sense of a wounding, of a big burden she had been carrying. Then I had the clear image of Our Lady of Guadalupe. (This is an image of Mother Mary that is especially beloved in its native Mexico. Claudia was born in Mexico.) I explained that I love Our Lady, and Claudia said she did too. Then Our Lady said to me, "I have her back." I did a double take. Did I hear that correctly? But because it was so clear, I repeated the exact words to Claudia, whereupon she cried even harder. Once she had collected herself, she told me that while she isn't religious, she had prayed just yesterday, asking Our Lady of Guadalupe to "have her back like she used to do." Now the unusual wording made sense to me. Our Lady said it was time for Claudia to do again what she did as a child. I asked Claudia if she worked with energy when she was a child because that is the hit I got. Claudia said she used to lay her hands on people and heal them, and she just knew what to do. She cried some more and was incredulous. I know her head was spinning. She was *beside herself—excited and her heart was blown open—her heavy burden exposed and released.*

Claudia left the house as a beaming, transformed young woman! What I found most intriguing was that even if the biofeedback monitors registered only small physiological changes, all the people reported experiencing significant changes in their body and their sense of well-being. These ranged from relaxation and expansion of the energy field to the presence of angels and guides, vibrations, chills, peacefulness, changes in light and colors, and so on… Once again our spiritual reality has superseded our scientific ability to prove it.

DNA—Our Link to the Cosmos

Awakening the Grail Codes was a mystical, spiritual event to which our cells or DNA seem to respond. This makes sense based on new scientific understanding about how DNA operates. The conventional view that all the instructions for our physical form and development are neatly preprogrammed into the sequences of our DNA is being rewritten. Science is now showing us that cellular control is not embedded in the DNA.[15] It is perhaps helpful to think of human DNA as receivers of information, like tiny satellite dishes to the cosmos. Bruce Lipton, PhD, author of *The Biology of Belief,* states: "Biological behavior and gene activity are dynamically linked to information from the environment which is downloaded into the cell."[16] The cell is programmed by something outside itself. He compares DNA to the key in a car, which cannot drive itself. What Lipton calls the biology of belief is that the body responds according to how the environment is *perceived*.

We know that the DNA continually interacts with the environment, receiving input and making adjustments based on the information. But what do we mean by the environment? Is it just the immediate vicinity? No, not at all. The environment from which the DNA can receive input is the entire universe—irrespective of time and space! In particle physics the idea of such massive, cosmic interconnectivity is called nonlocality. It means that particles of matter are so completely entangled with each other that they connect through all space and all time. In other words, something is everywhere at the same time. It is clear that in addition to the matter and energy that comprise the universe, there exists an invisible element that produces instantaneous coherence and communication throughout the cosmos.

What this means is that our body, through the mechanism of our DNA, is programmed to receive information from anywhere and everywhere. It is important to note that the programming, or information storage, of the cosmos doesn't occur in any one place; it is holographically distributed throughout. Said another way, our DNA strings access universal wisdom that is enfolded into the very fabric of existence. Erwin Laszlo in his book *Science and the Akashic Field: An Integral Theory of Everything* calls this interconnected information realm the Akashic field. What appears as separate in our reality is in fact interconnected. The great quantum physicist David Bohm postulated that the explicate order—the separate-appearing reality—is a projection of the invisible, but more fundamental implicate order, in which everything is a flowing, unified whole. The nonphysical implicate order can be likened to a spiritual template for the physical reality.

If the entire universe *can* be accessed from anywhere in the hologram, what determines what *is* actually accessed? If we go back to the metaphor of our DNA as satellite receiving dishes, what they download is dependent on what satellites they are tracking. The frequency range that you normally operate from determines what you track and therefore what you can access from the host of possibilities. If, for instance, you are very three-dimensional and spiritual growth is not of interest to you, your vibration will be centered in the 3D world. Consequently, your

DNA will receive cosmic imprints mostly about the 3D world. As you grow spiritually and play with higher states of consciousness, which correlate with higher vibrations that hold more energy, your DNA will be attuned to cosmic information that is much higher, broader, and different than before. So the DNA itself receives, repatterns, and translates multidimensional cosmic information into input to which your physiology can respond. Perhaps the 97 percent of the DNA that doesn't carry instructions—that has sometimes been referred to as "junk" DNA—is actually functioning as multidimensional antennae.[17] Simply put, how your DNA is attuned will determine what it can take in. Everyone's DNA has the potential to take in everything, but it may not be tuned to those frequencies or dimensions yet.

DNA, Thought, and Language

So here's the next logical question: "How *do* we influence that tuning?" The answer came to me from my spirit guide Mark as I spoke about DNA in Stockholm in 2007:

> *You are influencing it now with your intention. Intent is how it changes, and that is all. That is why it's so magic. Your intention focuses the DNA's receiving abilities. When you set the intention to grow, all of a sudden your DNA attunes to growth; the right teachers show up, the right books show up, and your friend says exactly the right thing that you needed to know. As you get that level stable and you set the intention to grow further, your DNA will find another satellite to attune to that is even higher, so you will get more and more and more. Your intention creates the new reality from the range of infinite possibilities. DNA is very*

important in creating your reality and it does it by responding to your intention. Many people think that the new energies that are coming in are the things that change the DNA. It is not so. The new energies that seem to be coming were always here. It is just that your intention has enabled your DNA to focus on those new energies now. You are actually more of a creator than you think and it is your DNA that creates through intention.

Researchers are finding what mystics, healers, and shamans have known for ages: that we are programmable by words, language, and thought. Linguists found that our genetic code follows the same basic rules of grammar and syntax as all human languages. Therefore, they concluded that languages are an intrinsic reflection of our DNA. Further, language can influence the DNA and genetic information. Russian biophysicist Pjotr Garjajev, exploring the vibrational behavior of DNA, found that indeed, "Living DNA substance (in living tissue, not in vitro) will always react to language-modulated laser rays and even to radio waves, if the proper frequencies (sound) are being used. This finally and scientifically explains why affirmations, hypnosis, and the like can have such strong effects on humans and their bodies. It is entirely normal and natural for our DNA to react to language."[18]

Beyond conscious programming of our DNA with words, language, and sound, our cells respond to the ever-present electromagnetic field that enfolds all things—from atomic particles to galaxies. We find that DNA is not only a passive responder to influences outside the cell, but DNA also exerts its own magic. The Russian researchers noticed that "DNA can create disturbance patterns in a vacuum, in effect producing magnetized wormholes." Wormholes are microscopic tunnel connections between "different areas of the universe through which information can be transmitted outside space and time. The DNA attracts these bits of information and passes them on to our consciousness."[19] This process of hyper-communication can explain such phenomena as telepathy, precognition, and channeling.

In a similar study, quantum physicist Vladimir Poponin found that DNA when placed in a chamber of randomly moving photons, has an organizing effect: "The presence of DNA had strongly organized the light waves into a coherent pattern... The presence and potency of this effect was vastly beyond what would have been predicted from mere chemical principles... Most astonishingly, when the physical DNA was removed, the photons remained in an organized pattern, a 'phantom DNA effect.'"[20]

In summary, Poponin's discovery of a multidimensional or quantum field around DNA—a field powerful enough to change matter—could be the link between our cells and universal consciousness—our body and our soul.

DNA and the Quantum Field

In 2006 I channeled information from Mark regarding the role of DNA and the quantum field in human consciousness evolution:

1. *In the current state of human consciousness evolution, the first changes are in the electromagnetic field, not biological or cellular changes. The "spin" of the field becomes set up differently. The field is the canvas on which life is painted.*

2. *The second step in human evolution is the entrainment of human consciousness to the new field. Be the consciousness. Become accustomed to moving around in this new realm,*

leaving separation and entering the vast consciousness of communion.

3. After human consciousness has been retrained into the new field and has established strength and self-perpetuating power, the third step begins. It is cellular electromagnetic transformation supported by the resonance of human consciousness to the new *field.*

4. *The fourth step is when cellular physical matter changes in alignment with the new electromagnetic cellular changes. This is where the DNA shifts—in accordance to the cellular and electromagnetic changes.*

5. If you make changes first in the DNA, they cannot be supported by the field. Lasting changes reverberate from the highest realms all the way to the cellular structure. Once the cellular structure is encoded with the higher field, then it is easier to change your human emotions and mental patterns. These change automatically when the make-up *and foundation of the DNA in the cells have shifted.*

The field is a vast information-laden holographic collective that gives rise to form. Physicist David Bohm, writing in *Wholeness and the Implicate Order,* suggested that, "all ordering influence and information is present in an invisible domain, or higher reality, and can be called upon in times of need." Mystics call it "the void," or "infinite potential." We might call it consciousness. Physicist and author Amit Goswami concurs: "Everything starts with consciousness. That is, consciousness is the ground of all being. In this view, consciousness imposes 'downward causation.'"[21]

Let's relate what we have just covered regarding the properties of DNA and its connectivity to the quantum field that underlies everything, with the words channeled from Ashtatara—the queen of Atlantis when she came through me in Malta to awaken the Grail Codes (Chapter 3). You can see that her words echo poetically what quantum physics has discovered scientifically:

> ...*The world is nothing like you think*
> *You cannot think this world.*
> *I have too much to say, but perhaps I speak*
> *better without words.*
> *I carry with me...a field of awakening*
> *that requires no words...*
> *The grail you seek cannot be understood,*
> *but known only through your heart.*
> *The Grail Codes are in you...asleep in you.*
> *and you have called me to awaken them.*
> *It has started.*
> *The awakening of the codes has started.*
> *You will not feel them.*
> *You will not see them.*
> *You cannot study them.*
> *Only your heart knows them...*
> *I am she who has awakened.*
> *You are they who have awakened.*

By reading these words, by doing Soul Body Fusions on yourself, you are intending for your DNA to awaken, aligning itself with a quantum field that is new to human consciousness. You intend that your soul transforms your life at all levels and in unseen ways with the highest possible outcomes.

Intention

Author and mystical explorer Carlos Castaneda wrote about intention: "In the universe there is an immeasurable, indescribable force which shamans call intent, and absolutely everything that exists in the entire cosmos is attached to intent by a connecting link."

As stated in Chapter 4, I believe that Soul Body Fusion works so simply for three reasons: 1) It is our natural state, 2) It uses the aligning power of intention, and 3) It occurs through the principle of resonance.

Let's first look at the power of intention. Intention is focused awareness, and we know from quantum physics that awareness changes reality. Lynne McTaggart, author of *The Intention Experiment,* wrote that "Recent discoveries in frontier quantum physics provide evidence that our world is highly malleable, open to constant subtle influence… Intention appears to be something akin to a tuning fork, causing the tuning forks of other things in the universe to resonate at the same frequency."[22] In short, intention is the dial with which we choose what we want to connect to and be associated with.

Professor emeritus at Stanford University William Tiller, PhD, and others have proved, in experiment after experiment, that intention works regardless of distance. This easily explains the fact that results from Soul Body Fusions done remotely are as effective as those in person. A surprising outcome of the distance intention experiments was the discovery of intention's lingering effect on the environment. Graham and Anita Watkins, from the Foundation for Research on the Nature of Man, found that a mouse placed on the spot on a table where another mouse had received a healer's intentions would revive more quickly. Along these lines regarding SBF, a woman re-experienced the same strong sensations a few days later when she sat in the same chair as she had used during the Fusion.

A key tenet of quantum physics is that the act of observation alters matter. Subatomic particles only exist as a wave of probability until they are observed or measured. You might say they exist in a virtual reality, in a sea of potentiality. Observation or awareness collapses the wave function into a singular existence, actually bringing the particle into being, as opposed to just *potentially* being there. So whether you call it awareness, attention, or focused intention, it is consciousness that creates and directs our material reality. Manjir Samanta Laughton, MD, in her book *Punk Science,* put it this way: Consciousness is fundamental to matter and not the other way around.

All of this goes to remind us that intention is much more than a positive thought or statement. It directs the immense resources of the universe to specifically support our requests. Following are two examples of the universe using its resources, and humor, to meet an unspoken intention.

I was shopping for ingredients for one of the few things I cook—Mexican quiche. In the produce section I picked up all the fruits and vegetables for the meal, then made my way to the exact opposite corner of the supermarket to get the required milk, cheese, and eggs. At the dairy section I suddenly remembered, "Darn, I forgot a red pepper." I wasn't looking forward to retracing my steps all the way back because of my forgetfulness. As I turned to the dairy case to choose the cheese I saw… right at eye level… proudly sitting between cheddar and swiss… a single bell pepper—not green, not yellow—but *red*! I chuckled my gratitude to the universe as I plucked the solitary vegetable from its most unlikely perch, where it clearly sat waiting for me!

Another example comes from Michel in the Netherlands: Upon completion of a spiritual training course to learn to help souls easily cross over at the time of death, he added this to the menu of healing services offered on his website—the price, a steep 2,200 Euros.

Soon after, while he meditated, a spirit being came to him, asking for help to cross over. Michel was hesitant because he was taught to only work with souls he knew, and he didn't know this being. However, the being was insistent that it wanted assistance, so Michel relented. "It was a lot of work," Michel told me later. "It took most of three days and a half to do the 'dreamwalk.'" That could be the end of the story—a good spiritual deed done, another soul helped. However, Michel's story had a most remarkable twist. When he next checked his bank account, there was exactly 2,200 Euros extra!

Wayne Dyer describes the magic this way: "Activating intention means rejoining your Source and becoming a modern-day sorcerer."[23]

Resonance

Since resonance is one of the three main factors behind why Soul Body Fusion works so easily, let's take a deeper look at it. Resonance literally means "re-sound," or echo. It was first recognized by Galileo Galilei in 1602 in his investigation of musical instruments and the swinging of pendulums. Galileo noticed the tendency for two pendulums in proximity to move into the same swinging rhythm. Scientifically speaking, it is a sympathetic vibration between two or more interacting wave functions. For resonance to work there must be a continuous exchange of information between the two. As in the case of two pendulums, each of them communicates with the other as if to say, "I am here in my swing. Where are you?" Then each adjusts itself based on the continuous information it is receiving. What is interesting in the example of the two pendulums is they move into exactly the same rhythm or period, but in antiphase—180 degrees opposite to each other! In a way, their swings move in a manner to perfectly counterbalance and complete each other. This could be what happens in a Soul Body Fusion. The soul and body communicate through the electromagnetic field and adjust their intrinsic vibrations to create a new pattern that is mutually uplifting and completing.

In Soul Body Fusion our physiology begins to resonate, or synchronize, with the higher frequency of our soul, entering into harmony with it, causing physical shifts, and in some cases instigating a process of healing in our body.

Biophotons: Light in the Cells

Before leaving this chapter on science, there is one more topic that is relevant, given some of the more common physical sensations people report when they have a Fusion. Many experience what feels like deep cellular changes: light, bubbles, vibrations, buzzing, tingling, heat, tickling, popping, opening, releasing… and so on. My curiosity to learn what this might be led me to the emerging science of biophotons.

German biophysicist Fritz Albert Popp proved that all living cells emit tiny bursts of light called biophotons, which are weak electromagnetic waves. Taken together, they create a measurable electromagnetic field, or aura, around all life—plants, animals, and humans. In addition to emitting light, the DNA in the cell's nucleus actually absorbs and stores light. The continuous release and absorption of biophoton light creates a web of connection and communication between cells, tissues, organs, and the entire body. This biophoton field has consciousness like properties that might be the interface to the nonphysical world of our soul. This could be the basis of the traditional Chinese concept of ch'i and the Indian yogic idea of prana: both basically describe the flow of life force energy through the body.[24]

It is interesting that there is a difference in the quality of light emitted depending on the state of the cell: a healthy cell radiates coherent light (having laser like properties), while a diseased cell radiates chaotic light. A disturbance in the body's electromagnetic energy field caused by the frequency patterns of our thoughts and emotions can cause a breakdown in our ability to stay healthy.[25]

Although I have no way to test this right now, my hypothesis is that our intention in Soul Body Fusion to invoke and merge more completely with our soul connects us to a higher frequency, more coherent part of our multidimensional self. The tremendous electromagnetic field of our soul communicates through the biophotons to the cells, enabling them to raise their frequency, strength, and coherence. This results in an immediate increase in the vitality of our cells and an increase in our overall life force energy. Sometimes this induces our cells to release toxins, making some people feel sick, achy, hot, or uncomfortable during or following a Fusion. At other times people feel lightness, warmth, tingling, and opening, which are likely indicators of our cells taking on higher electromagnetic frequencies or light. Our luminescence becomes a galactic conversation whereby each little synapse of radiance moves holographically through the universe and is responded back to in return.

We have already seen, in the research by Valerie Hunt (Chapter 1), that increases in a body's frequency range are indicative of spiritual growth from mere materialism to a higher level of personal development. The higher the frequency, or vibrational pattern, we consistently hold, the easier it is for us to get and stay healthy and experience well-being, happiness, peace, joy, and bliss. Our greater light keeps us strong and supports us in having a positive impact on others and our planet.

Chapter 9

Other Helpful Ideas for Spiritual Growth

You must begin awakening to different realities in order to activate the expansion of consciousness that will allow you to know… the creative, infinite energy that you call God.

-Mark

Now that you've learned Soul Body Fusion and have hopefully practiced it with others, here are some additional ideas and tools that I think you will find helpful for your spiritual growth and balance. Over the years these ideas and techniques have been a huge gift to me.

Multidimensional Consciousness

Embodying the higher vibrations of your soul opens the doors to experience expanded states of consciousness that may have been closed before. You may notice shifts in your awareness, or increased intuition and other spiritual gifts beyond the third-dimensional limitations.

Since the late 1980s I've been working with my cosmic guide, Mark to explore, map, and navigate the higher dimensions of human consciousness. His first words through me in 1989 foretold the work we would do together:

> *I am Mark. I have traveled a great distance in terms of energy. I come to bridge a gap between dimensions unknown. My world is on the other side of time, the other side of matter as you know it... You must begin awakening to different realities in order to activate the expansion of consciousness that will allow you to know... the creative, infinite energy that you call God.*

Mark began to transmit energy meditations that lifted groups of students to the various levels above the physical plane. Each higher dimension includes all the dimensions below it and has increasing power, as well as infinite intelligence and scope. We notice that in practical terms it is easier to change lower dimensions by first effecting shifts in the higher dimensions. That is why the incorporation of your soul—a higher dimension of you—can have such an immediate impact on your 3D life.

We create our lives from the level of our primary awareness. Therefore, the world we experience is a direct reflection of the fundamental state and structure of our personal consciousness. When our consciousness is primarily linear and singular, then our world is linear and limited. When our consciousness becomes multidimensional and fluid, our world is experienced in a multidimensional way and we are able to see creation as infinitely sourced.

Following is the descriptive map Mark has given us over the past two decades to help us understand where we are going as we expand into higher states of being. I share it so you can have some signposts for your own spiritual growth. Of course, dividing the world into discreet layers is for teaching purposes only. Consciousness itself is indivisible; dimensions are nested and interconnected with each other. This map represents *experiential* levels of consciousness rather than dimensions that are scientifically discernible. Please note that different teachers have different descriptions of the dimensions.

The First, Second, and Third Dimensions: 3D Physicality

This is the physical, material, tangible level of form. Both time and space are linear here. Our personal focal point is our body, personality and ego. We experience it through our five physical senses.

The Fourth Dimension: Waves and Energy

If the third dimension is the particle aspect of matter, the fourth dimension is the wave aspect. It is less tangible and includes energy, light, vibrations, frequencies, color, sound—anything that is primarily wavelike. It can be experienced through our senses and intuition. Fourth dimensional (or energy-healing) modes such as acupuncture, Reiki, and homeopathy are effective in influencing the denser physical world of the first three dimensions.

The Fifth Dimension: Geometry and Symbols

Mark teaches that this dimension is expressed through symbols, codes, geometric shapes, and other forms of mathematics. As such they are still within the space-time continuum, but they tend to be the bridge to the unseen worlds. For example, the healing energy of Reiki was first given to Dr. Mikao Usui (the originator of Reiki healing) in symbols. Reiki initiations and healing rely on the use of symbols to transmit the energies. In a personal example, when I received a solar initiation in a meditation in Peru, I felt it as thousands of packets of codes, or symbols, coming into my cells—the Sun Disc codes. Finally, as covered in this book, the power that activated our DNA to open the way for Soul Body Fusion was given to us as unseen symbols—the Grail Codes. Tremendous meaning, power, and healing are possible from the fifth-dimensional level of symbols, shapes, and codes.

The Sixth Dimension: Magnetic Reality
This is the first of the higher dimensions that exists beyond the limits of space-time. It can be described as unity consciousness—a space of infinite expansion. It is a space of *being*, not *doing* which contains no form. One way to enter it is by moving your awareness to your heart and then letting it expand into infinity. This is the level of consciousness where I go to experience oneness. It feels like a magnetic space of quiet power without force or movement. Mark calls it the "Miracles Space." Our weekly Mark study group worked for over two years to find and hold this high level of consciousness. It felt as if our brains needed to be significantly rewired in order to maintain our identification with this state.

The sixth dimension feels so unbelievably different from the first five dimensions. I was so thrilled to finally get to this rarified state that I promptly began to use it to pray for the world. Thunk! I crashed out of it—dropping back to the 3D world. Each time I started *doing* something, like praying or thinking, I was ejected. I learned the hard way that it is a place of being, not doing. This is further proof that the higher states of consciousness do not require—in fact, they do not tolerate—effort.

The Seventh Dimension: Holographic Consciousness
To enter this dimension, you must experience a fundamental shift out of singularity and linearity, until you feel that your existence is centered everywhere, holographically—as is all else. The seventh dimension is a vast, infinitely connected world that

Mark refers to as God Consciousness. It feels like you've tipped the scales into an exquisite, multifaceted space where you feel both unity and diversity. Mark explains that "all-that-is evolves when any part of it evolves. God is not so much a being as the composite and interaction of all." The seventh dimension is the experience of the scientific principle of nonlocality. A possible indication that you've entered the seventh dimension is that you visualize a single eye, or perhaps the esoteric symbol of the eye in the pyramid. It represents an all-seeing perspective that is everywhere at once.

The Eighth Dimension: Quantum Consciousness
Arriving at the eighth dimension is about traveling into the world of probable existence—the threshold beyond black holes. Your first experience is likely to be incredible speed or shifts that end in a void of unmanifest but knowable potentialities. Scientists can extrapolate measurements for our known universe and can account for only about 3 percent of existence; the remaining 97 percent is sometimes called dark matter. This is the space of consciousness that can lead to quantum shifts in your life. Mark is currently teaching us how to magnetize new and different realities and precipitate them into physical reality.

This multidimensional consciousness work has been an ongoing, interactive experiment over twenty years with Mark as our guide. The importance is for those who are drawn to such cutting-edge exploration to gain in skills and abilities and create consciousness pathways for others to follow. Our stability in the higher dimensions creates a critical mass that stimulates others to open to their potential. Such personal exploration requires one to be solidly connected body and soul.[1]

---

[1] Mark's courses are available on www.JonetteCrowley.com.

Advanced Spiritual Gifts

Quantum consciousness makes possible skills we've mostly associated with gurus and masters: levitation, bilocation, materialization, and teleportation. Here is an amazing story from a young Finnish man who has a powerfully angelic nature. I first met Vesa in early 2008 at a Soul Body Fusion workshop in Helsinki. He was touched deeply by the words and energies of Ashtatara. This sent him on a quest that changed his life.

> *I had the feeling in my heart I was going toward a more magical life. At the weekend course it happened: the final soul blessing, heart shocking—Soul Body Fusion. I had never experienced anything like it—being home in my body. "Welcome home, my light, my sunrise, power and love, wisdom and peace," I repeated. I was a reborn and redone man. The pain of the past was gone. After hearing Jonette speak of Malta, I knew my next step was to read this book (Jonette's book: The Eagle and the Condor) and to have a look at Malta. I entered "Malta" on Google. "My God, this is the place," I thought. I canceled a spiritual trip to India and booked a ticket to Malta.*

Note: Vesa moved to Malta in 2008, and in 2011 he still lives there.

> *A year later, I flew to the Netherlands to attend another SBF class in The Hague. It was a huge confirmation that I am on the right track. Then, in 2010 I arranged a holiday in Romania, where Jonette was teaching Soul Body Fusion. I enjoyed the workshop—even though this was my third time in the course. This time, in Ro-*

mania, I experienced an energy rotation like all the old was sucked out of me and new energy inserted. It felt like a fresh start.

Back in Malta just a couple of days had passed. Around midnight I got a call from a friend. I went to meet him, even though my tiredness was taking control of me. After two hours I told him, "I need to go home," and I called a taxi to meet me in front of a nearby McDonalds. I took a step to walk there and I heard my heartbeat and a bang. As I walked forward I froze... I didn't recognize the street! "What! Where am I??? How did I get here?" Confused, I broke down and cried. I was somewhere I had never been and I didn't know how I got there!

Then my phone rang and the taxi driver asked, "Where are you? You're not in front of McDonald's." I saw a street sign and told him the name. "Listen, that isn't even in the same town. Do I send you another taxi?" In a matter of seconds, I ended up on a street several villages away from where I waited for the cab!

I arrived home with the feeling of panic, horror... I spontaneously teleported! I screamed at the mirror, "Who am I? What happened? Who took me? Can it be real?"

Guess it is time to accept a new gift, though I'm afraid to go to sleep. I lie now with my clothes on, with my passport, my money, and my phone; my backpack tied to my foot... "What alien planet will I end up on? Or will I land in the middle of the Atlantic Ocean?" I was even more worried to shower... ending up naked with shampoo in my hair, in a place like the middle of London.

Some weeks later, I began consciously practicing to teleport. I said out loud, "I want to teleport now!" A blue mist shot around me; a line came up my spine to the heavens. I was shaking like never before... rapid eye movements... every cell was out of control... like I wasn't here anymore. I realized I didn't have control of what was happening or the location I was going to. Panicked, I shouted, "I cancel. I cancel. I cancel!!!" I collapsed on the floor. "I need more practice for this."

After a few more self-training sessions, I was able to move around inside my house. At night a light illuminates my room and I have visits from Poseidon and Ashtatara... fusing and melting energy into me. I feel such great promise and adventures of magic to come.

From a conventional perspective, the idea of teleportation is unbelievable. Yet, the esoteric literature has always included such tales. The book series that initially opened my mind to the idea is *The Life and Teachings of the Masters of the Far East*, by Baird Spalding, first published in 1924. Be warned. If you attend three SBF courses who knows what spiritual gifts might open up. I believe we will see more such spiritual phenomena as humankind continues its advancement.

Himalayan Heart Activation

Since an opened heart space is so important in reaching multidimensional awareness, I share the Himalayan Heart Activation—a gift we brought back from Nepal. Not far from

Mount Everest stands one of the world's most spectacularly beautiful peaks, Ama Dablam. As you remember from Chapter 2, in 2003 I was guided to lead a group to the Himalayas to do a special process for healing the Earth of negative energies. As we meditated in a yak pasture next to Nepal's highest monastery we experienced an activation in which our hearts awakened to a higher level of existence.

Demonstration of a Himalayan Heart Activation. Fig. 9.1

These higher frequencies serve as a catalyst that automatically activates your heart and the hearts of others. One way to experience this directly is with a partner. To do this, each of you places your left hand over your heart and your right hand over the other's left hand. This creates a circuit of mastery in which the highest in you both is activated and exchanged. Sometimes you can feel the moment the energetic link clicks into a circular flow. The experience is a deeply profound heart-to-heart connection. Stay in this connection for a minute or two, drinking in the beautiful peace that is magically created. The intention of spreading this heart blessing is all that is needed. People don't need to know anything about its origins.

If you don't have someone near to connect with, go ahead and put your left hand on your heart and your right hand out as if you are giving to and receiving from the world at large. Because this simple blessing has proved so extraordinarily powerful, I have made a short video about the Himalayan Heart Activation that you can find at www.JonetteCrowley.com. You *really* can get it from the video! A man who translated for me in Finland watched it and, feeling kind of silly, put his left hand over his heart and his right hand out to the computer screen. He immediately felt a huge opening and shift in his heart! He laughed as he told his story to our audience in Helsinki. What have you got to lose? No one will see you.

Absorbing and Radiating Process

In addition to the Himalayan Heart Activation, another way to quickly experience a higher state is the Absorbing and Radiating Process. You might think of it as a new way to pray. If you are like I am, your prayers include a lot of asking. Granted, the asking maybe quite selflessly intended—asking help for others. Nonetheless, our prayers are generally a laundry list of requests great and small. This sort of praying keeps us in a mental, thinking mode, preventing our soul from soaring to an exalted state of letting go and communing with the Divine.

White Eagle suggested we try a different approach. For the first five or ten minutes, let your thoughts be quiet and simply absorb light, grace, peace, high frequencies, love. No thinking. No asking. Imagine you are a sponge for the highest possible goodness. Seems easy enough, right? I thought so too, but I failed miserably the first time. For about a minute I was fine, easily absorbing love and light—a peaceful smile on my face. Then, in an instant, the spongelike absorbing ceased and I was releasing it all out again. Mindfully, I brought my concentration back to absorbing. That lasted another minute or two before the direction again changed from receiving to giving. It was as if my heart's energetic valves were set to automatically give, making it a struggle to receive. Could this also be true for you? Please put down the book and try it right now. Keep absorbing goodness, light, peace, wisdom, and abundance until you've done it for five minutes straight, without popping back into the outflow mode.

Once you've mastered absorbing for at least five minutes, you're ready for the radiating phase. Now it's okay to let the flow be from your heart out to the world at large. Radiate as the sun does. Its life-giving heat and light are merely by-products of its essence as a giant chemical furnace. Don't push or choose where the outpouring should go. Stay in the radiating phase for at least five minutes.

Then open your eyes and take note what has changed. For me, even though I struggled at first, I was amazed that this simple process had catapulted me above the density of mass consciousness. It was as if I was in a high, light, rarified atmosphere looking down at the brown, dense smog of normal human consciousness. It is a spectacularly easy way to lift above the confines and thought forms of the masses. Try it. You may never go back to the old way of praying again.

Body Diagonals

This tool helps bring left/right balance to you. In Soul Body Fusion and other spiritual practices we are most often focused on the vertical aspects of our growth: aligning our chakras along the midpoint of our body, bringing our higher self down through our body into the earth, and so on. At times you may be surprised to find that the more you reach up to your higher aspects, the more unstable you become. You might notice that you are emotionally fragile or your body is out of sorts or clumsy. Often we are so focused on the vertical movement of energy that we ignore the diagonal flows—the connections that balance our left and right sides. There was a time when my body was so out of balance that my left side felt solid and stable; my right side weak and skittish. The voice of my inner guidance was quick to offer a simple visualization.

Imagine an "X" going through your body, connecting each shoulder to the opposite hip, intersecting approximately at your solar plexus above your navel. I imagine the "X" has no beginning or end. Use your inner sight to take stock of the width and density of each diagonal. One line may be thick and solid, the other thin and broken. Instead of fixing the broken, weak diagonal line, put your attention on the stronger. Then hold the intention that the weaker diagonal copies the thickness and strength of the stronger one. Wait without doing anything. Check in with your mind's eye every few minutes, watching for the moment when the two diagonals look or feel the same. Use your imagination. Once they're both solid and equal, you're done.

I've shared this need for diagonal realignment with several healers who now end their energy sessions by opening the flows between their client's shoulders and opposite hips, or shoulder and opposite foot. It seems to make a concrete and perceptible difference in body balance.

Cosmic Battery for Harmonizing

The Cosmic Battery is a visualization tool to bring calmness, peace, and order. While SBF changes you by making your divinity more present, the Cosmic Battery affects the world around you. It can create a space for healing, manifesting, and accepting. In the same way that a car battery stores incredible amounts of energy and power, even when nothing appears to be happening, the Cosmic Battery concentrates various bands of vibrational energy in an organized, still, and elegant way.

First visualize a flat plate, a flattened disc of spiraled energy—like a phonograph record but infinite in all directions, spiraling from the inside out. Imagine an infinite number of these flat spirals stacked one upon the other. Since everything consists of vibrations of different frequencies, imagine that every frequency in the universe has its own place, just as yellow has its address between orange and green on the spectrum. This cosmic sorting will bring an instant sense of calm, a feeling of order brought to chaos. This Battery can be used for any situation that requires harmonization and flow. I usually imagine that I am in the center of the stack of infinitely extending spiraled plates.

The Cosmic Battery visualization allows the inclusion of all energy. Nothing is bad; nothing is separated out.

If there is something you want to change or experience from a higher level, absorb it into the Battery. Perceptions, relationships, and situations may change. You are calmed. As you expand your visualization of layers and layers of infinitely thin spirals you expand the overall volume of energy you can hold.

I have a friend who wanted a used hunter-green Jaguar sedan with white leather seats… and it had to be an incredible deal. She was very specific. Whenever she thought about her future car, she harmonized with it by encircling it with the spirals of the Cosmic Battery. She wasn't too surprised when a local car dealer phoned her to say, "Ma'am you're never going to believe this, but someone just traded in the car you want and it is in your price range. I've never seen a car like that on this lot before."

A Nurse Uses the Cosmic Battery with a Mental Patient

This is a story submitted to my newsletter many years ago by Karen Lambert, a psychiatric and critical care nurse working in a psychiatric ward for the involuntarily committed in an inner-city Philadelphia hospital. I include it not only as an illustration of the impact of the Cosmic Battery but also as an example of a mental disorder that clearly had a spiritual cause and responded magically to a spiritual, energy type of healing. Below she tells the story of Robert:

> *I had a very psychotic, violent patient Robert, who had begun to follow me around. Finally, he came up to me*

and said, "My guardian angel will help you."

I called Jonette to talk to White Eagle for guidance on what was happening and how I could help this patient. White Eagle assured me that Robert was correct and that his angel, St. Christopher, was indeed ready to assist in some breakthroughs. White Eagle explained that fragments of Robert's past lives as soldiers were attached to him and that much of his extreme violence stemmed from that. (Robert was permanently institutionalized for mental illness and had served time in jail for a stabbing.) White Eagle said that the past-life fragments needed to be put into their own context and released. He also asked whether Robert had a problem with fire. I wasn't aware of any.

Back at the hospital the next day, the energy of the ward was extremely chaotic, so I went into my small office and used the Cosmic Battery techniques to stabilize it. The room instantly felt harmonized and clear, as stable as the rock of Gibraltar.

I then invited the Robert in for five minutes of therapeutic conversation. After sitting down and absorbing some of the calm, blended energies, he started to scream "Fire! Fire! Is there a fire in here?" He was panicked. A couple of aides ran up to restrain him, but I waved them away. I wasn't exactly sure what to do, but I remembered that White Eagle had asked if Robert had a problem with fire. Noticing that the voice, inflection, and mannerisms were not that of Robert at all, I calmly told him, "There is no fire. It is 1992. You are

Robert and you are in the hospital. I am your nurse."

"How did it be 1992?" Robert asked with a distinctly British accent.

"Are you a soldier?" I said, my hair standing on end as I addressed this past-life fragment.

"Yes, my name is Tom." He then told me his regiment number.

I continued to maintain the high vibrations in the little room while I addressed Tom, the past-life personality, telling him he needed to go back where he belonged. Tom left and Robert returned. Robert expressed awareness of the soldier and wanted to know what happened.

I explained that fragments of his past lives, that were soldiers, were coming into his current awareness as Robert. He accepted this explanation, even adding that the soldiers looked like ghosts.

"You mean they have to go back to history?" he asked.

(Understand that this man is very dysfunctional and has a severe mental disorder. It was rare for him to ever string a sentence together, much less understand a new concept. The fact that he was so lucid with regard to this situation was more than remarkable!)

"Yes, they have to go back to history," I said. *"How?"* he asked.

"You tell them to go back to history and your guardian

angel will help us."

We were interrupted and our time together was over for that day.

Several days later I again used the Cosmic Battery to set up harmonized energies in the small room. I invited Robert in. As soon as he got in the energies, his voice, inflection, grammar, and vocabulary changed. I knew we were dealing with another past-life fragment.

He was very upset and cried out, "You don't know what they did to me! They hung me!"

In dealing with multiple personalities, we are trained to speak to the dominant personality. I did the same here: "I want to speak to Robert."

The personality of the current Robert reappeared, and I asked, 'Is there another soldier here?'" "Yes." Robert replied. "Do I tell him to go back to history?"

"Yes, and your angel will help you, Robert," I said. "Go back to history!" Robert shouted out loud.

Instantly the feeling of the room shifted and Robert was calm. I believe that the Cosmic Battery removes time-and-space barriers and helps us to blend and accept all energies into harmony. That is why the fragments could easily revert to where their energy belonged.

"Is the soldier gone?" I asked.

"Yes, but what about Bobby? he asked, meaning his juvenile current-lifeself.

"Bobby is a part of you that needs love. He is supposed to stay here with you. So we have to love Bobby and Robert."

After this final clearing of the soldier-past-life fragments, Robert's medical records showed a dramatic shift in every way. Before I began working with him spiritually, he had been in our unit five weeks, with no improvement. Now the nurse's notes showed that he was more coherent, and involved with his environment. When he was with me and I did the Cosmic Battery, he was always totally coherent.

One situation that shows just how much he improved was when another patient threw a chair at him in the dining room. Normally, Robert's reactive violence would erupt and he would have to be placed in restraints. On this day he simply said to the other patient, "Sit down and stop that!" Everyone in the dining hall was amazed! Because of his rapid improvement, plans were made for his discharge. This was less than a week after he and I started working together, based on White Eagle's advice.

I wanted to make sure that Robert was clear once and for all of his past-life influences, so I asked him, "Are the soldiers coming back or are they really gone?"

Robert answered, "The soldiers are gone, but they left a gift for me. They told me they are going for now but that when I die I can be with them and Jesus."

Personally, I had a hard time accepting that a healing miracle had really occurred, though Robert clearly took it in stride, asking if I wanted to join him for a soda. He was discharged the next day. He has been monitored weekly on an outpatient basis and has maintained his coherence and his level of mental health.

This example of healing a chronic mental disorder through intention and visualization gives pause for us to consider just how much mental illness is spiritually based and can be spiritually healed.

Your Angels and Guides

Beyond tools, techniques, and visualizations is an entire realm of help, just waiting for you to call on it. I'm talking about spirit guides, angels, fairies, even gnomes and nature spirits. Don't believe in them? No problem. They believe in you!

Several years ago because of financial worries, I had lost my sense of inner peace. With my sister Erin, I visited a tranquil Buddhist stuppa (temple) nestled in the pine-covered mountains of northern Colorado. As we sat on cushions on the intricately inlaid marble floor, I meditated and prayed for help in lightening the load that was weighing me down so heavily. Immediately I saw a vision of myself walking on an ever-inclining path, burdened by cares and worries represented by a huge, unwieldy load of firewood. Pieces of wood were falling everywhere as I struggled to carry them. The pile in my arms was too high to see clearly where I was going. Yes, the vision was a snapshot of exactly how I felt—hopelessly oppressed and very sorry for myself.

As the inner tableau continued I struggled to move forward under my burdens. Not able to see ahead, I glanced to my side.

Quietly walking next to me, waiting for me to glance her way, was an angel—smiling at me and effortlessly pushing an *empty* wheelbarrow!

The angel and the wheelbarrow. Fig. 9.2

Soul Body Fusion can expand your state of awareness so that the previously inaccessible world of spirit guides and angels becomes more present in your life. Here I have a humorous experience to relate from Marie, my friend and organizer in Sweden. Marie has always felt innately guided, as if she just didn't need a spirit guide. She and I flew from Stockholm to Skåne, in southern Sweden, to teach a weekend Soul Body Fusion workshop. We were house guests of Eva, a new friend, who kindly opened up her hundred-year-old farmhouse for us to stay in. Before we retired to our part of the rambling country home for the night, Eva warned us, "Don't worry if you see my ghost. He has been here for decades and he is harmless." Neither of us thought much of it.

The next morning Marie was awakened by a presence, speaking clearly into her mind: "Perhaps this isn't a good time to introduce myself. My name in Enoch."

"Go away," Marie responded sleepily to the intrusion as she shooed the ghost from her bed. "I'm trying to sleep." As Marie and I were getting dressed, she told me of her visitor: "The ghost came this morning and introduced himself. He said his name is Enoch."

"That wasn't a ghost, Marie!" I quickly exclaimed. "Enoch is a *really* high archangel!"

"Oh, no, I chased him away!" Marie said, aghast. "I thought it was the ghost! I hope he understands and comes back again… he was very polite."

Enoch did come back. He now gives Marie clear instructions on health, diet, work, travels, and spiritual growth. He gave her a message for all of us: "The more you take care of your body, the easier it is to connect with your soul. Please listen to your guide or inner voice to learn what the best food and exercise is for you."

Even if you have never connected to the higher realms before, Soul Body Fusion can give you a step up.

Chapter 10

Resources and Frequently Asked Questions

You are asked to be the creators of a template of humankind—a template where the DNA is fully opened, where all of who you've been is remembered and that is just the beginning for who you can be.
                                                            -Ashtatara

Resources

Soul Body Fusion is a work in progress. As you add your energy and wisdom to the field, it will continue to expand—perhaps in unprecedented ways. We have information on courses, certified teachers, and events, as well as links to practitioners, videos, and discussions on our main website, www.SoulBodyFusion.com. We will have links to similar websites in languages other than English as they are added. In addition, we have designed a line of beautiful Solar Grail jewelry that helps hold the energy of Soul Body Fusion. You can go to the Center for Creative Consciousness at www.JonetteCrowley.com for information on other courses, products, and spiritual adventure tours.

I have endeavored to adhere to the No Rules philosophy as much as possible. I encourage *you* to find creative ways to use and test SBF and to report back the results to others on our SBF Blog or Facebook page. We would appreciate having results submitted involving the use of SBF in areas of need such as autism, addictions, depression, eating disorders, pain management, ADHD—any number of issues that plague our society.

Guidelines

Once you have read this book, you can do Soul Body Fusions on yourself and others. You are encouraged to make it part of a healing or coaching practice… or whatever you do! Whenever you use the words Soul Body Fusion® on your website, business cards, or flyers, please always include the ® symbol, as it is a registered trademark of the Center for Creative Consciousness.

For further depth and support in using Soul Body Fusion, I encourage you to attend a course taught by one of our international team of Certified Teachers. There is tremendous value in working on SBF with a group in a class or retreat setting. Experiences are shared and the energies are compounded. If you would like to become a Soul Body Fusion Certified Teacher, check out the training schedule on our website. We ask you not to teach SBF unless you are a Certified Teacher.

Frequently Asked Questions

To help you feel more comfortable in doing Fusions, I've gathered together some common questions and answers. As you practice Soul Body Fusions you will develop your own expertise.

How do I combine Soul Body Fusion with other healing modalities?

The beauty of SBF is that it works through a protocol of no outside interference. Therefore, it can combine with and empower any other healing modalities—medical or alternative. However, when you are first learning SBF, so that you can understand its power as a stand-alone tool, I suggest you do it on its own without combining it with other energy work. Once you understand how little you do and how much can happen, you may even reassess whether other approaches need to be included. Always use your intuition. Of course, continue any medications and doctor's orders.

Does it always work?

Why do some people improve from cancer, fractures, and depression, while others do not? This is the million dollar question. The answer goes back to "your soul is in charge." What happens and how is scripted by the soul. You are ceding your ego's idea on what the outcome should look like to the soul's longer time frame and infinitely wiser perspective. The view I hold is that no matter if I feel physical changes or not, SBF is without doubt moving me forward in my spiritual growth and my soul's highest path. Here is a tool that has no downside risk, which in many cases has a huge upside potential—why not do it?

Sometimes it works quite obliquely. Maybe you don't feel any changes directly, but you happen to pick up an article that has the answers you've been seeking. Who is to say that your soul didn't set up that synchronicity?

Can it harm me or cause me to grow too fast?
Since in Soul Body Fusion there is no interference from a healer, or anything other than your soul, it is my experience that it can do no harm. Yes, people may feel sick or emotional after a session, but the nature and pace of the growth is firmly in the hands of the soul. (Hmm, do souls have hands?) The highest self is the wisest governor possible for growth. This accounts for such variance in Fusion experiences—from sudden, nearly cataclysmic opening of the kundalini to changes so slow and subtle as to appear almost nonexistent.

What is the difference between soul and light body?
Here is a great definition of light body from Sanaya Roman and Duane Packer—light body teachers with whom I have had the pleasure of studying: "Your light body is an energy body that exists at a higher level, closer to your soul, than your chakras. Your light body opens doorways to the higher realms of light, such as the soul plane."[26] I feel that it is a vehicle to get me to the higher dimensions.

Am I taking away someone's karma if I heal them?
Let's go back to our comment: "I can't mess it up, because I'm not doing anything anyway." You are not the cause of the changes. Your role is not as a healer or advisor. Through your intention you help issue an invitation to another's soul to permanently harmonize and integrate. Everything that happens is under the jurisdiction of that person's higher self. What I see as the overall objective of SBF is to raise us to a higher vibration so that we transcend our personal karma.

Can you do it on pregnant women and babies?
Yes, of course. I would encourage a pregnant woman to receive Fusions, with the intention that she and the baby integrate with their souls as fully as possible. If the fetus is less than seven months along, the Fusion will be primarily magnetic. Between seven months' gestation and birth, the Fusion will be more electric. (See Chapter 4 for details on this.) But none of this matters to the facilitator, because the baby's soul will fuse in the perfect way for it. I've heard beautiful stories of a mother who did SBFs on her child during the entire pregnancy. As soon as her son was born, she placed him on her belly and gave him his first Fusion as an independent being. After the trauma of giving birth, the new mother could also certainly benefit from a loving Fusion.

…On people who are dying?
We can't presume to know the process or timing of a soul disengaging from the body and moving into the afterlife, or between-lives. Having the body aware that the soul is present might be helpful to make the transition as conscious as possible. However, if the soul is already on the way out, it will reject the intention to fuse.

Can the Fusion ever be broken?
I asked this same question of White Eagle. His channeled response was that if there is a major trauma, it is possible for the soul connection to be diminished. But short of that, Fusions are permanent. He suggested the process of doing three Soul Body Fusions over three weeks to strengthen the results. (See Chapter 5 for details.) In my experience, the process of three Fusions has significantly more impact than a single Fusion. Remember, any or all of the Fusions can be done remotely.

Can you do it too much?
I don't believe so. If you are pushing too hard from your personality, your soul will ignore it and will do only what is right for your greater good. Your soul is a subset of the infinite spirit, so there is no end to how much you can harmonize and expand into spirit. I do remote Fusions on people whenever it pops into my mind to do so, especially if they are going through tough times.

What if the person gets a headache?
In doing SBF with her son, Lili in Romania discovered something interesting. He complained of a headache and a pressure in his head, as if the crown chakra was blocked or not big enough for all the soul's energy to enter. She asked him to receive the energy into his upturned hands and then direct it to his head—like a reverse circuit. When you do this, it feels like a stopper is pulled out from the head.

People often sense a band tightening around their heads, or pressure in the Third Eye area. When that happens, I usually remind them to expand their aura in order to hold more. I also suggest that they imagine the incoming energy moving all the way through to their feet.

What do I do when the person receiving SBF is stuck and the energy is not moving?
It is not unusual for people to experience energy that begins in their head but gets stuck along the way down. Usual blocks are at the neck, hips, and knees. Remind them to "stay in their body." If you are facilitating the Fusion in person, your downturned hands resting on their hands generally directs the energy down into their lower legs and feet. If that still doesn't get the flow going, I sometimes gently put my feet or toes on the tops of their feet… of course, only if I am just wearing socks, not

shoes. My feet on theirs tend to ground them and bring their awareness and energy all the way to their feet.

You say that it is more than a healing tool. Please explain.
Consider that your soul is much more than your body, so the possible changes you can experience encompass everything about your life—not just physical. A Fusion moves you further along the continuum to your greatest potential. For some it brings more clarity about their life purpose, for others more personal power and self-confidence. It can enable forgiveness or release self-sabotaging habits. It can help you understand and process difficult life circumstances, open your heart, awaken your spirit, increase your self-expression… all so much more than mere physical healing.

What happens in your relationships when you change?
On the one hand, sometimes when you change no one notices. You go back to your friends, family, and colleagues, and they still interact with you out of the same vision and pattern they have always held for you. You may be amazed to notice how many people stopped relating to you years ago; they relate and react only to the concept they have of you. So it will be up to *you* to relate to them differently.

Now that you have a new vibrational field that extends around your relationships, people will move to where they are comfortable. While some may move closer because they appreciate the new brilliance in you, others may feel threatened. For them, your new grounded power may cause them to see their own issues more clearly, and they may distance themselves. Stay aware of what is happening and always go back to your truth: What do *you* feel? What do *you* need to do differently? The truth is always in your consciousness. Part of the magic of this sort of work is how easily relationships can heal. People have shared amazing stories of forgiveness, acceptance, and improvements in relationships.

When I'm doing Fusions on others, how do I protect myself against negative energies?
Your radiance is your best protection. I channeled Mark, whose response to this question was simply, *"Does the sun need sunglasses?"* When you are fully present in your body, overflowing with your soul's love and light, negativity cannot reach you. In the past, much of our growth was individual, occurring in our own protective igloos. The next level of human evolution must be collaborative, with no shields. Shields between us cannot be sustained in this new world, because the field we are creating is beyond such barriers. The decision to protect against negativity confirms the reality of negativity and makes the separation concrete. Rather than separating, absorb their energy into yours… the acceptance transforms everything. Protection is the antithesis of transformation. You can still choose not to spend time with certain people, but be sure the decision isn't charged with the emotion of judgment. That which is separated cannot be healed. It is the breaking down of the separation between our spirit and our body that gives Soul Body Fusion all its power of transformation. Remember the muscle testing example I used in Chapter 8? The bottom line is that when you are positive and grounded in a feeling of wellbeing, no matter how much negativity surrounds you, it cannot impact you.

Sometime after I had a Fusion, I went to a healer, who said I must be very tired because my body and soul weren't together. Did I do something wrong?
SBF is a continuous, nonlinear process. You can't do anything wrong, but it works differently for everyone. There are many

levels of soul potential to be integrated. Your Fusion was working first on the unseen magnetic and electrical levels, before any physical changes manifested. Trust your own instincts and trust the process.

What if I never feel anything or see any changes?
True changes are not just those you feel in your body. The canvas of Soul Body Fusion is your entire life. To see real changes, step back and notice whether clarity comes faster to you, whether emotional grace and stability are easier to find, whether you are less impacted by drama and negativity, whether you are more accepting and forgiving. Perhaps you smile more. Perhaps you have a better job or take a nice vacation… These could also be soul's work. Your highest self works silently and powerfully through channels you will accept, giving you what you are ready to receive.

When I do a Fusion on myself while reading this book, with whom am I resonating?
You are primarily resonating with your soul/higher self. However, reading this book puts you in touch with the collective, or morphogenetic, field of all who have reached a higher merged state—whether through SBF or through other spiritual practices. The intention that you set by reading this book resets your satellite dish—to use a previous analogy—to receive from higher sources.

Answers Channeled from Mark

How is my soul related to overall consciousness?

Soul is a fluid subset of consciousness. At any given moment there are no firm boundaries between your soul and someone else's soul, the Earth's soul, the world's soul, or the galactic soul. There is just the seamless field of consciousness. However, for the purposes of communication and interaction, we infer demarcations we call soul.

How can I tell if I'm growing and making a difference on the planet?

*Sometimes when you make the greatest difference in the world or when you grow the most, you see it the least. This is because you are growing without another frame of reference. As you grow, you are growing your world. If any of you has been in a hot-air balloon, the most amazing part is the silence. Since you are being carried with the wind, there is no feeling or sound of wind resistance. If you did not have the Earth and its markers below to see how fast you are going, you would perceive no movement. Sometimes the difference you are making is so profound that you are the balloon **and** the wind.*

How are my thoughts limiting me?

Let your experiences direct your thinking rather than your thoughts constrain your experiences. Your thinking is the vessel that needs to expand. As you trust your experiences, you begin to seek out different experiences and let them redefine your thinking. Thinking is not what it has been cracked up to be, although it has created the culture that you have now. The imbalance of thinking compared to receiving true wisdom could cause this culture's downfall.

Thinking is a predecessor of duality because you have a thinker and you have a thought, so there are always two. The dimensions beyond thinking are connected to universal wisdom. Wisdom isn't a thing; wisdom is part of the overall being, part of the same fabric as you. Oneness is predicated on the wisdom model, but the thinking model engenders duality. Duality is not bad. First and foremost, it ensures survivability. After survival you are invited to the next level of evolutionary growth, which is thriving, which is spiritual illumination, which is connectivity without conflict.

It feels like I am softer and more polished. What is happening?

You have been given a key to unlock the next door. How far you move through it is up to you. Your energy is softer and more stable. You will find it hard to have the same emotional highs and lows, as you no longer need that amplitude for your recreation. You have an expanding sense of presence and wisdom. You will be less driven and have less need for conflict. Softness, kindness, fineness, and self-assurance will become more commonplace in your life. This resonance will go out into the world and help refine those things that can be refined, and push away those things that refuse to be refined. The world is becoming a truer place, more true to its essence and less needing to prove existence by power and drama. In many ways it is the transition from masculine to feminine—the hard to the soft.

I can feel something happening in the core of my physicality, what is it?

Your physical particles are becoming excited, so they have more power and energy in them; this means they spend more time in the quantum universe. The quantum aspect of your physicality can't be measured, but you can feel it in your sense of aliveness. Most of the time people receive or import the feeling of oneness, for example, "Ahh, I was bathed in oneness." The switch is for you to export oneness so that oneness isn't something you receive, but something that moves from you as cause. Oneness is born and is amplified through you to humanity. You are becoming more multidimensional—more quantum—and at the same time becoming a stronger individual. You might say a quantum individual. Once you are reconnected to the wholeness, you can powerfully, wholly, healthfully be an individual. You are no longer broken.

There are times when I'm just exhausted and can barely function. Is that part of the changes that are occurring on Earth?

You are spiritual transformers. You are active bringers of high frequencies. You step down these higher-dimensional vibrations so they are accessible to others. You open doors so the rest of humanity can benefit from your willingness to explore. If you don't recharge, your battery gets drained. You recharge by connecting to your soul, by connecting to your soul group, by connecting to that which gives you joy. It's not always spiritual. If you love to cook, cooking a fine meal can recharge you. When you connect to that which recharges you, even if it's for a few minutes, you will find that the exhaustion can be reversed fairly quickly.

What is the galactic perspective of these times?

From a galactic point of view, humanity and Earth are becoming more integrated. As you open, there is a wealth of possibilities, wisdom, power, strength, and miracles that will pour into humanity. The growth is exponential and is well supported throughout the galaxy. The human experiment is the spiritual unfolding of a species that sees itself as individual. Most other intelligent species operating as individuals see themselves as collective.

Humans operate and see themselves as individual but don't quite grasp the collective. The growth in awareness of the collective into humanity's individualized perspective brings a huge possibility to the entire galaxy. This opens doors or time warps that facilitate the speed of energy and wisdom exchange as you tap into different levels of knowing. There is occurring a basic updating of humanity's operating system—away from polarity and competition to oneness and generosity. The shift is not time-based. It is a dimensional shift. The first step in any of this is to connect to your own body.

What can help us deal with all the changes that are happening?

This is a time of ambiguity. You will need to learn to surf on the waves of confusion. The future won't become more certain; you just become better surfers. Certainty and predictability are aspects of a linear world. A multidimensional world is about impossibility, miracles, and inexplicability. It is not certain, but it can certainly be comfortable. It's more comfortable in a different way—it is connected to infinite wisdom rather than the comfort that comes from what is circumscribed and defined. This is the time to redefine the nature of the comfort that you seek—seek the comfort of the open sea, not the safe harbor. The seas will call you; the vastness will call you forward. You will be built for uncertainty. When you are built for uncertainty, you will seek it out because it is uncertainty that enables possibilities. So many people pray for a life that they can handle. Why don't you pray that you can easily handle more?

Mental confusion always precedes a new paradigm. People would rather believe what they know than believe what is true but is unknown. You who are reading this book are yearning for truth beyond beliefs. In the conundrum of the unknown is the unanswerable, and the unanswerable will lead you to truth. Truth expands to the extent you prove to your own greater self that you can hold it. Once you integrate it, you get higher and higher levels of truth. The invitation is for you to supersede yourself.

Chapter 11

More Mysteries Revealed

You are progressing on an unprecedented path. This is what you choose and have always chosen. Confusion is part of the luggage of a pioneer. So, let confusion open your curiosity and curiosity lead you to your power. You will not have all the answers; you will never have more than half a key. Go forward anyway.
                                                                            -White Eagle

The Lightning Initiation

Now that you understand a little of the science underlying Soul Body Fusion and have answered some questions, let's go back to the mystical aspects of this adventure. For me, the greatest personal gifts from SBF are enhanced perception and spiritual abilities. I hold more and higher energies, I am more clairvoyant, and my spiritual skills have intensified. Of course, when our powers increase, so do our responsibilities. We are thrust in situations that test us, challenge us, and make us use what we have learned. No doubt you will also experience this as you continue doing Fusions.

Remember when Ashtatara, the goddess of Atlantis, came through me, awakening the Grail Codes—our DNA? Her last command was "Do not call me back!" She was not one to be disobeyed, so reluctantly I have never called on her again.

However, she has come to me several other times… only at her bidding. The next time she showed up, I was surprised, as I was doing a channeled reading from White Eagle for Berdine, a friend in the Netherlands. Berdine had just asked White Eagle about the strong connection between her, me, Evalyn (who sensed the dragons in Malta), and Yolanda (who has accompanied me on all my spiritual journeys). All three were present in Malta when Ashtatara first came through. As I channeled for Berdine we both felt that the energy and words were not White Eagle's. The words were poetic. The energy was powerful yet feminine. We had the tape recorder running.

Daughters of Isis, daughters of Venus,
sisters of the sacred ways,
mothers of the times before,
birthers of the times to come,
holding patterns for perfection,
holding true to wisdom's light,
opening the chalice of the Holy Spirit,
parting darkness into light.
Weavers of a greater pattern,
you walk with lightning on your shield.
Daughters of Isis and Venus,
a greater future is revealed.
I am Ashtatara,
proclaiming the time—
the deliverance of the goddess,
bringing with me a pattern of transformation

> *discontinuous of the past.*
> *These times will mark*
> *a strong foothold of the goddess*
> *into a large circle of hearts.*
> *I invite humans to give up*
> *the vision of what you think you want,*
> *so the vision of possibilities may be unlimited,*
> *to hold in your hearts the reality*
> *of a discontinuous transfiguration.*
> *This is a time of grail and goddess.*
> *Shalom.*

The beauty of her words kissed our souls. We were more than ready to "hold in our hearts the reality of a discontinuous transfiguration." However, one phrase struck me the most and begged to be more fully understood: "You walk with lightning on your shield."

I was reminded of the highest initiation a shaman can have—higher even than a solar initiation—and that is the lightning initiation. In the Andes and other native cultures, when a shaman has progressed nearly to the pinnacle of abilities, he or she will go to the mountains and ask to be struck by lightning, either dying or becoming enlightened in the process. The risk was grave. A lightning initiation was not for the faint of heart.

That evening in meditation, I asked for the meaning of the phrase "You walk with lightning on your shield." In response, I experienced a jagged lightning bolt of white hot electricity in the palm of my right hand, and I sensed what it meant. The next day I gathered together the three other women whom Ashtatara had addressed: Berdine, Evalyn, and Yolanda. As a shaman, I called forth the lightning in my hand, placing my palm on the forehead of each of the modern priestesses. We knew this brought us to a higher level of power and mastery. The electricity I felt in my cells was physical evidence of an immense personal and spiritual shift.

Please note: the lightning initiation is not something you can ask for. You receive it when you are ready, and you will know. It isn't for everyone. You can be quite spiritually advanced and not receive this initiation, as it isn't on everyone's path. I can sometimes see that people are initiates, or have the capability to hold the power of the lightning initiation, by noticing an etheric lightning bolt on their forehead. I believe that when you are ready, Soul Body Fusion may bring you first a solar initiation, and then for some—a lightning initiation. You may feel it as searing electricity in your cells, or you will just know that you've moved to another level in your spiritual path of mastery.

Anne from Norway wrote to me of her experience when she first heard me read Ashtatara's words:

> *In a workshop in Oslo, Jonette was reading Ashtatara. I wasn't able to hear more than the first few lines. Suddenly I was hit by a cannonball of light. I could see it coming and it hit me in the center of my chest. I was thrown back in my seat. I started crying, with tears running down. At lunch I was disoriented and couldn't easily communicate. Later I felt electricity in my hands, and my heart was beating irregularly. If I had been in another setting, I would have thought I was having a heart attack.*

Anne and I both believe that in that moment she received a spontaneous lightning initiation.

Transylvanian Underworld Journey

As often happens, once we receive a spiritual gift and have integrated it, we are faced with a new mission, one that tests ours kill and mettle. My most intriguing spiritual mission came a week after receiving the lightning initiation in Amsterdam. It happened in Romania. I include this story because it was the next step on the path that surrounds my discovery of Soul Body Fusion. It is for those of you who are intrigued by spiritual adventure and secrets that are just beginning to be uncovered.

Cosmin was a sixteen-year-old high school student in Bucharest: a chubby, bespectacled youth in that awkward teenage period. My Romanian organizer Carmen assigned him to me for the week as my translator because "his English is great." Which it was. When I asked him how a boy from Bucharest learned to speak such good English, including American colloquialisms, he replied, "From cartoons." Cosmin—like cosmic—is also one of the brightest people of any age I have ever met. In the five years that we've been friends now, I am deeply honored to know him. His innate leadership and wisdom are rare in one so young.

He was a talker, enthusiastically sharing the history of his beloved homeland. Over lunch on our first day together he launched into a story with so many twists that I couldn't tell if it was fact or fantasy... hidden caves under the Bucegi Mountains in Transylvania, ancient tunnels to Egypt and Tibet, spy satellites, strange electromagnetic force fields, hidden technology left by advanced civilizations from fifty thousand years ago, psychic children, a high-level Mason, top-secret excavations by the United States military... He told me that these stories became known through several bestselling books by Radu Cinamar, published only in Romanian at the time. His conversation was entertaining but had nothing to do with me, or so I thought.

Cosmin was fascinated by the supposedly true legends of the hidden caverns and intrigued by my ability to channel and to travel through space-time. He felt certain that I had an important role to play in clearing the tunnels of negative power. I wasn't sure if this was something of which I was capable, or if I really wanted to do a shamanic journey into a mysterious underground world that represented a top-secret military project. Also, the only "facts" I had were the enthusiastic words of a well-read sixteen year-old. He was adamant that we should take the train to Transylvania so I could meditate in the Bucegi Mountains to find out what I could see with my spiritual vision. His earnestness was not merely that of a teenager. He acted and spoke with authority, tapping into power I had not seen in him before. I took notice of the shift and knew that my role was to follow his lead.

A blizzard shut down all options of physically traveling to Transylvania that late October day in 2007. Undeterred, Cosmin explained that he had prepared a ceremony so we could do the shamanic journey virtually, from my rented apartment in Bucharest that evening. Out of his student backpack, he pulled some crystals and a typed prayer that he said came to him the night before. Cosmin and I were joined by friends, Carmen and Mira. Candle light warmed our faces as we sat together on the floor. The wind roared, rain poured, and thunder rumbled. Even the lights in the apartment flickered on and off. In a setting that seemed right out of the movies, we did a special journey into the ancient tunnels. I admit that my doubts were strong throughout. Wasn't this just my imagination? Yet I trust that when I'm led to such unusual circumstances, nothing is lost by going for it—acting as if I know what I'm doing. Below is a (slightly abridged) transcript of the recorded words I narrated as my spirit journeyed into the caves and tunnels in the Bucegi Mountains in Transylvania. Cosmin read out his prayer, calling on the early deities of the area as well as Christian saints to protect us. In his invocation, he brought me to the door of the cave entrance and asked three times if I was worthy.

I began to speak:

> *I use the sign of the Lightning and ask to be deemed worthy to enter the fortress of night that protects the chamber below. I call upon the spirit of the White Brotherhood to light my way. I go with a pure heart. I walk with power. May the gate open. The gateway is in the seventh dimension. It is invisible to journeyers with less light. It is beginning to open. There is much chaos in the energy here.*
>
> *I have entered a room where goddesses stand around a fire. The entire place is illumined with light, not of the fire. The inner door cannot be opened by one alone, but must be breached by a consensus of high consciousness. When the goddesses are ready, we move through the mountain. The energy [beings] here feel sinister. We confront them, telling them to take their negative influence on the world away. The power of the light grows stronger; the darkness here grows weaker. We now see a tunnel with symbols along the sides of the walls. There has been a great deal of manipulation and negative influence from here toward humanity. The phalanx of goddesses moves through the tunnel to Egypt first, reclaiming it for the light, taking back the records. There is much healing. The beings here forgot about the power of the human heart united.*

They forgot about the power of the mountains and the stars. They forgot about the power of good. Now good reclaims the discs of remembrance. We call again the angels, the saints, the wise ones, and elders to move their energy and their light into these tunnels to reclaim again the discs of knowledge.

As a sign that it is done, a white she-wolf walks out of the cave with her pup. For this day, the mission is complete. Light has reclaimed the caverns of the underworld. A bolt of lightning marks the sign of an inner door. It is still closed, except to those initiated into its power. It is not for the common tourist. The Earth herself will feel this healing deeply. It is done, Shalom.

I ended my narration with the word "Shalom," which has become the signature closing for Ashtatara whenever she comes through. It was then that I knew that she was with me.

At the end, the four of us shared experiences. Each saw and sensed different things, which we pieced together. Cosmin felt that he followed me inside the caves. From a perspective behind me he saw the goddesses, the tunnels, and the symbols on the walls: "The white wolf was with you the entire time, protecting you. She was wary and alert, ready to attack if you got into trouble." I was grateful that the spirit world had had me covered with such a special power animal.

I had done this shamanic journey at the request of a teenager from Bucharest, a young man I had only known for five days… at least in this life. I didn't know what to believe—after all, how could it be real? I could stretch my imagination to believe in secret caves with advanced ancient technology, but tunnels to Egypt and Tibet—isn't that a bit farfetched? Or was it? Didn't the stone tablets that the German researcher Hubert Zeitlmair translated speak of a war in Atlantean times in which the Earth was honeycombed with tunnels, some passages leading from continent to continent? (Refer back to Chapter 3). What were the discs of remembrance? Why did I say those things?

The lightning initiation from Ashtatara was the key that supported this spiritual mission. I used the "sign of the lightning" and the higher vibration within me, which the lightning indicates, to gain initial entrance through the "fortress of night" that protected the inner chamber. In this underworld journey I also saw the power of the lightning when the goddesses sent light into the caves and tunnels to clear them. It was an explosion of lightning bolts that flashed zigzagging through the inner Earth's crevasses and tunnels. As in this adventure of mine, I believe that infusing our earthly existence with our higher dimensions, through tools such as Soul Body Fusion, gives us access to wisdom and opportunity that were closed to us before.

The next day, as the early winter storm still blew and blasted Bucharest, I flew home, leaving the mysteries of Transylvania behind for a future day.

Continued Adventures of a Spiritual Indiana Jones

The questions about this fantastic story of hidden caves with incredible technology, electromagnetic protective fields, and clandestine military activity still haunted me. For now the books by Radu Cinamar, which first brought the tale to light, were only available in the Romanian language. I would have to find other ways to get confirmation of the reality of the story.

In November the following year, when I returned to Bucharest to teach workshops, I was curious to learn more about the truth of these secret caves. Since the power of intention in my life is so miraculous, I wasn't surprised when, synchronistically, I met two men, on two separate occasions, who had been involved in different parts of the intelligence services in the Romanian government.

First, I did a White Eagle reading for a retired colonel in the Romanian military intelligence services. This coincidence made the hair on my arms stand up. In twenty years of readings, I don't ever remember a military man seeking spiritual guidance. Afterward we went to dinner together, enjoying the conversation and sharing a bottle of wine. After a while I just *had* to ask him about the secret caves in the Bucegi Mountains.

"I have kind of a James Bond question for you" —I opened the questioning, launching into the story. "I heard from a young man who read some books about secret tunnels and caves… and the involvement of some of the highest degreed Masons, the Illuminati…"

He interrupted, "What's the question?" "Are there tunnels?" I got right to the point.

"Yes. Your government knows about them. You can't go there. It is all well protected."

"But I *did* go there… in a shamanic journey. I saw… well, I hate to say it… evil… dark energies. Why is the government there? Do they have spiritual intentions?" I queried.

"They want technology. It's always about technology." "Cosmin says there are discs, codes and records… ," I continued.

"The Masons can journey there too. But they don't have the codes… the right frequencies,"he volunteered. "But I do! I went there!" I blurted out—in retrospect, not the smartest thing to admit. I can blame it on the wine.

The ex-military guy was quick to jump in: "Can you initiate me with the codes?"

I did notice the mark of the lightning on his forehead. "Yes, if you are ready for it your soul will take the initiation. You can't just ask for it... Who made the tunnels?" I continued.

"Another civilization."

"I think it's from Atlantis," I added my opinion.

"I don't know. I'm a very rational man." Then the conversation took a different turn: "Let's take a possible scenario. You work for the CIA or Israel. You're trying to get information from me by establishing a relationship."

I replied, "What if *I'm* a target?... because I know this place?" I added the insight: "The military will never get the real information. They will be cursed... sickness, death, accidents."

"What about the 'dark forces'?" he asked me.

"They are surprised we're coming. They've been operating for thousands of years with impunity. We humans have had war and struggle and poverty and it isn't entirely our fault. We've been somehow influenced energetically from these places," I summarized.

My new friend had a surprising and heartwarming response: "I want to change the morphogenetic field of Romania and create the potential of transformation."

I was excited that he saw his mission in terms of changing consciousness. Smiling, I gave him a high-five as we left the restaurant.

The second confirmation regarding these secrets came a few days later during a workshop. Cosmin was my translator, so he and I told the class a little about our inner journey to the caves the previous year. A gentleman attending the workshop came up to me later and identified himself as having worked in intelligence for a Romanian government agency. I remembered a comment Cosmin had made about one of the secret tunnels going to Tibet through Baghdad, so I had a question for this man:

"They say there is a tunnel from Romania that goes through Baghdad to Tibet. Do you think this is the real reason behind the United States being at war in Iraq?"

"Yes," he replied quickly, "and it is the reason the Russians and now the Americans are in Afghanistan. There are lots of secret tunnels under Afghanistan. In Romania everything about the tunnels has the very highest security clearance—Level Zero. Only the top people in the government know the details."

I asked myself, "What is the purpose for my being led to this unique information?" Of course, I don't know where any of this will lead, but I am fascinated by the possibilities. Synchronicity has always been my silent spiritual partner.

Transylvania Sunrise

Many of my questions were answered when Radu Cinamar's popular Romanian exposé about the discovery and contents of the secret caverns became available in English—*Transylvanian Sunrise*. The author was briefly given access to the mysterious chambers so that some basic information about the discovery would be made public. This purportedly true story is rich in spiritual wisdom, intrigue, paranormal abilities, and fascinating information left hidden by advanced Earth beings from eons ago.[1]

It was exciting to finally read details about the ancient chambers and holographic records stored there, and to corroborate the stories I had heard from Cosmin, and through my own inner journey. I immediately phoned Radu Cinamar's American publisher, Peter Moon of Sky Books. I shared with him my unusual shamanic experience and we talked about the

---

[1] The sequel, *Transylvanian Moonrise: A Secret Initiation in the Mysterious Land of the Gods*, is now available in English.

discovery.

One thing I found especially interesting in the book, in part because it confirmed an aspect of the shamanic journey I did into the mountain in 2007, was that there was indeed an electromagnetic protective shield that could only be breached by persons with a specific, high vibration. (In my case it was the lightning initiation that encoded me with the vibration.) Only one person—a man with significant paranormal abilities—had been able to move through the shield unharmed. It was he who opened it for the military, and later for Radu Cinamar.

Cinamar writes that the gigantic chambers are magically self-illuminated. I had noticed that too, in my journey. They hold unbelievable technology, including machines that create holographic projections to communicate a vast array of information on physics, cosmology, technology, astronomy, religion, biology, life on other planets, the history of Earth, DNA analysis of life forms, and much more. It is a great universal library, a hall of records. I assumed this is what I called the "discs of remembrance" in the narration of my foray into the caves. Data found in the main "projection chamber" on the location of the stars relative to Earth enabled military scientists to figure out that the advanced technology was placed in the Bucegi mountains about fifty thousand years ago. Radu Cinamar witnessed some of the information-laden holographic projections while he was in the caverns. From what he saw, his summary was that 90 percent of what we've been taught about the history of humankind is wrong. The myths and legends are closer to the truth, including the legends of Atlantis and Lemuria.

What I take from this incredible discovery is a reminder for all of us to remain curious and open, to trust our instincts—even when they lead us down nontraditional paths. Our job is to raise our personal vibrations, growing our spiritual skills and gifts.

The transformation of current conditions on Earth requires the transformation of the consciousness of individuals. When we are fully awake, exercising our personal and collective free will, we can't be manipulated or lulled into accepting less than our divine greatness. It is time to reclaim this birthright, opening the doors to a new era of spiritual truth and knowledge.

I believe that there are other amazing, hidden treasures, time capsules of truth that will be uncovered as humanity is ready. The Tibetan priest T. Lobsang Rampa wrote in his book *The Cave of the Ancients* in 1978 about a similar cave, also containing advanced technology, hidden in Tibet. His descriptions parallel features of the Bucegi find. Rampa described a soft, silvery light that was everywhere in the massive chamber: "Strange machines crammed the place… The light drew in upon itself… then it formed and remained in spherical shape… Within the sphere of light we saw pictures… we actually *saw* the events."[27] How better would you describe holographic images such as Cinamar witnessed projected from machines in the mountain?

Lama Mingyar Dondup, who was with the first group to find the Cave of the Ancients in the Tibetan Himalayas, told the author, Labsang Rampa: "Thousands and thousands of years ago there was a high civilization upon this world." He spoke of similar chambers hidden beneath the sands in Egypt, one under a pyramid in South America, another in Siberia: "Each place was marked by the symbol of the times, the Sphinx… These secret chambers were concealed by the peoples of old so that their artifacts would be found by a later generation when the time was ready."[28]

Even Edgar Cayce, the famous American "Sleeping Prophet," who received remarkably clear information in a trance state, told of an ancient Hall of Records hidden beneath the paws of the Egyptian Sphinx.

The Tibetan Lama's statement about a sphinx marking the

spot of buried ancient artifacts is prophetic. Directly above the secret halls and chambers in the Bucegi Mountains is a sphinx! The Romanian Sphinx is one of the most-visited tourist sites in Transylvania. There is just so much we don't yet know.

A Spiritual Pilgrimage to the Sphinx

In September 2010, Cosmin, the young man who started me on this exploration, insisted that I come to the Bucegi Mountains of Transylvania to hike, meditate, channel, and do energy work on the very mountain that contains the ancient caverns. Cosmin, eleven spiritually gifted Romanian women, and I donned our hiking boots and our backpacks for a two-day spiritual adventure. We understood that we couldn't get anywhere near the place where the military had their secret operations, but our goal was to hike and meditate together on the mountain under which the complex lies—the mountain marked by the Romanian Sphinx. We wanted to bring light, balance, and peace to the area.

The fierce autumn wind blasted through the mountains, forcing the authorities to close the easy way up—a gondola to the top. Plan B was an hour and half drive on winding, bumpy dirt roads in taxis to a trail head. Along the way we drove through rugged forests, out of which emerged weathered locals in woolen hats, baskets brimming with mushrooms they had collected. We didn't see any bears but knew they were around, feasting before their long winter's nap. The sun was at the crisp, clear angle that makes the fall so special.

Our hike that first day took us to one of the many caves in the area. This one—Ialomița—was guarded by a monastery. In Romania, churches, convents, and monasteries were sometimes built in caves. For more than an hour we walked inside the limestone chambers, climbing ladders, marveling at stalactites and the golden colors of the minerals. The air was wet and earthy. Past a small underground lake, we came to the inner sanctum. Here we meditated, calling on the feminine energies of Mother Earth to bring light and peace to whatever secrets the military were uncovering in the nearby mountain. I asked for all of us to receive a Soul Body Fusion for strength.

The climb up the mountain was longer and more difficult than we anticipated. Our stamina and our water bottles ran low. Cosmin directed a few of the group to a natural spring to refill the canteens for all. The others stumbled wearily through the rapidly descending fog, trying to make out the shape of the simple hut on Omu peak that would be our refuge. It seemed that the moment we found the hut, night slammed into the mountain on the back of an impenetrable, cold mist.

Among the dozen or so other hikers who shared the shelter was an author, Octavian Sărbătoare, who was an expert in the ancient spirituality of the area… coincidence? With gloved hands holding cups of hot tea in the flickering light of candles, we talked about the mysteries in the mountain below and the universe at large. Octavian was pleased to hear that the mission of our little band was to bring light and the feminine power of balance to the military discoveries in the mountain. He was astonished when I told him I channel White Eagle. With excitement he shared, "I've been coming to this place for decades. Today as the taxi driver let me off at the trail to start my hike, we both saw a white eagle in a treetop! Neither he nor I have *ever* seen a white eagle in these mountains before!"

The next morning was cold and wet. We wrapped up in blankets and huddled together in the bunk room to meditate and to hear from White Eagle. Here is part of his message.

> *This mountain is a place where spiral energies emerge from the Earth. It is a place of fire and light. You are invited to become like the fire, asking that your mistakes and darkness be burned away. Let a solar fire burn within your core, moving up and down your spine. At this moment of light you become the circle of fire. You are not alone, for many groups are called to sacred circles of service. The message of the mountain is that truth can be covered but never destroyed. Patience and right timing will always uncover hidden darkness. As you journey here, aspects of your hidden self become uncovered to truth. You arrive burdened and you leave naked. The mountain asks you for courage because the circle of fire is not for the coward. Humankind has become cowardly because it has become fearful. If you choose to help become redeemers, you must first be courageous in your heart. Compassion requires the highest courage. If you have compassion without courage you are pretending.*

Octavian, who knew the mountains well, led us through the morning rain to the peak of Kogaionon, where for thousands of years people have been constructing simple altars. These mountains here have been seen as sacred for millennia. Princes of old were initiated into special spiritual knowledge at the mountaintop near the Sphinx. Our group gathered white stones, placing them in the shape of a six-pointed star within a circle—the symbol of the White Brotherhood. The moment we placed the last stone, we felt the strong sense of spirit connecting heaven and Earth. It was as if our requests were heard and acknowledged. As we blend spirit and matter together through personal

Soul Body Fusions, we become better conduits for greater light to move through us into the Earth. We become the change we want to see in the world. (Thanks Gandhi.)

The spiritual adventure that brought me to the Romanian mountains will no doubt continue to unfold. I plan to bring groups there in the future to explore the area.

Chapter 12

A Call to Service

"Good times are to come when the moon is in full eclipse over the arctic. Then the difficult ride will slow for humanity. It will be a great time of healing and prevailing strength for the ones who so desire."
                                                                                    -Kelly

Heaven on Earth

In 2008 a young woman who had never channeled before received the message above. The full lunar eclipse she alluded to coincided with the solstice on December 21, 2010—a convergence of lunar and solar events that hasn't occurred for many hundreds of years. On this special day I was guided to take a group to the King's Chamber of the Great Pyramid at Giza, specifically at dawn and dusk. The Pyramid is a multidimensional gateway, an energy generator and magnifier. It was the perfect place to do a global Fusion—the joining of heaven and Earth.

Millions of people connected with us that day through meditation and intention. Energetically, we helped clear and lift human consciousness, creating a collective initiation for humankind. We established a high-vibrational "Initiatory Gridwork" that now encompasses the globe.

This was a celestial and terrestrial merging, a realignment with the forgotten aspects of human divinity.

You can utilize the Initiatory Gridwork to raise your own vibrations and multidimensional harmony by connecting to it through your intention. It is important to feel grounded and expanded when you do this, because the energies will be magnified as they return to you in waves. First, find a quiet place and focus on your heart until it expands into a space of oneness—that I call the sixth dimension. Then ask to connect to the highest aspect of the Initiatory Gridwork that you can reach. You might visualize gateways of endless ascending and descending triangles, creating a diamond matrix of light that anchors in new possibilities. With this opening, we have more spiritual help than ever before. Trust it. How it manifests is up to you.

During our time in Egypt, White Eagle told us: "The power will prove to be disruptive—in a good way, creating abrupt discontinuous transformation." Who knows if this energy work supported the rise of democracy movements in Egypt and the entire area, just a few weeks later? I do believe that as we answer the call to service—each in our unique way—we play a part in creating the world we would like to see.

An aspect of our ongoing service will be in relationship to the Earth. If we are disconnected from our own bodies, it follows that we are disconnected from the Earth and nature. I invite you to do Fusions for our Mother Earth. There is an intimate aliveness as form and spirit merge. At those moments a sacred alchemy is birthed that reminds us of the infinite intelligence of the universe. White Eagle was once asked, "How do we heal the Earth?" His response: "Your job isn't to heal the

Earth. Your job is to love her, and with that love she can heal herself." Isn't love, then, our only job?

There is an essence that has been missing—the actual presence of love as a creative, energized force, as the Divinity within us. We have *intellectually* understood the God within, but our bodies and atoms have not been attuned to receiving it completely. Love is more than a thought or emotion; it is an undeniable reality from which we can never separate. We don't *go* home. We *are* home. The new paradigm in human consciousness is unification based on love. In the past our unification was generally based on the need for protection. Through Soul Body Fusion and all the other processes you are drawn to, you are creating the foundation for a new humanity. It is part of an evolutionary impulse toward oneness.

We are building a new platform for existence moving forward. Instead of fixing the old shack… we are quietly building a mansion. While most everyone else is scraping, painting, and fixing warped floorboards in the old, we are constructing a high, stable place in new consciousness. When it is done, we'll go back to the ones with splinters in their hands and help them move gently forward. Let us envision together a world where we can live in a perpetual state of uncaused well-being.

I've been around the planet, activating elements of earth, water, fire, and air. You may ask, as I have, "Where is the last element—spirit—to be activated?"

It is activated in you. By you.

Bibliography

Aloisio, Francis Xavier, *Islands of Dream: The Temple of Malta—Hidden Mysteries Revealed*, Author, 2009.

Bartlett, Richard, *The Physics of Miracles: Tapping Into the Field of Consciousness Potential*, Atria Books, New York, NY, 2009.

Bohm, David, *Wholeness and the Implicate Order*, Routledge, New York and London, 1980.

Carroll, Lee (Kryon), *The Twelve Layers of DNA,* Volume 12, Platinum, 2010.

Chopra, Dr. Deepak, *Reinventing the Body, Resurrecting the Soul: How To Create a New You*. Three Rivers Press, New York, NY, 2009.

Cinamar, Radu (with Peter Moon), *Transylvanian Sunrise*, Sky Books, Westbury, NY, 2003.

Crowley, Jonette, *The Eagle and The Condor: A True Story of an Unexpected Mystical Journey*, StoneTree Publishing, Greenwood Village, CO, 2007.

Dyer, Wayne, *The Power of Intention: Learning to Co-create Your World Your Way,* Hay House, New York/London, 2010.

Goswami, Dr. Amit, *Physics of the Soul: The Quantum Book of Living, Dying, Reincarnation and Immortality*, Hampton Roads Publishing, Charlottesville, VA, 2001.

Goswami, Dr. Amit, *The Quantum Doctor: A Physicist's Guide to Health and Healing,* Hampton Roads Publishing, Charlottesville, VA, 2004.

Green, Glenda, *Love Without End: Jesus Speaks*, Spiritus Publishing, Sedona, AZ, 1999.

Hawkins, Dr. David R., *Exploring Consciousness*, Shift Magazine, 2009.

Hawkins, Dr. David R., *Power vs. Force: The Hidden Determinants of Human Behavior,* Hay House, Carlsbad, CA, 1995.

Lipton, Dr. Bruce, *The Biology of Belief: Unleashing the Power of Consciousness, Matter, & Miracles*, Hay House, 2005.

Mattulich, Dr. Liana and Paperny, Dr. David, *Journey to Awareness and Beyond: With Modern Technology and Ancient Wisdom*, Xlibris, 2008.

McTaggart, Lynne, *The Intention Experiment*, Free Press, New York, NY, 2007.

Newton, Dr. Michael, *Destiny of Souls: New Case Studies of Lives Between Lives*, Llewellyn Worldwide, St. Paul, MN, 2001.

Pearl, Dr. Eric, *The Reconnection: Heal Others, Heal Yourself*, Hay House, London, 2001.

Philip, Brother (aka George Hunt Williamson), *Secret of the Andes*, Leaves of Grass Press, Bolinas, 1976.

Rampa, T. Lobsang, *The Cave of the Ancients*, Ballantine Books, New York, 1978.

Samanta-Laughton, Dr. Manjir, *Punk Science: Inside the Mind of God*, O Books, United Kingdom, 2006.

Schwartz, Dr. Gary E. R. and Russek, Dr. Linda G. S., *The Living Energy Universe*, Hampton Roads Publishing, Charlottesville, VA, 1999.

Spalding, Baird T., *Life and Teaching of the Masters of the Far East, Volumes 1-5*, DeVorss & Co., Marian del Rey, CA, 1924 (Renewed 1964).

Index

A
Absorbing and Radiating Process 173
abuse 60
activating 12, 14, 15, 17, 19, 161
addictions 4, 61, 129, 186
Ashtatara 30, 31, 32, 34, 35, 36, 37, 39, 41, 42, 43, 71, 139, 157, 185, 200, 201, 202, 206, 207
Asuara Sidha 34, 35
Atlantis 24, 25, 28, 29, 30, 34, 35, 37, 39, 43, 157, 200, 209, 211, 224

B
biofeedback 148
biophotons 162, 225
Body Diagonals 175
Bucegi Mountains 203, 204, 208, 213
Burrows Cave 28, 29, 31, 34, 37, 224

C
cancer 129, 131, 132, 133, 134, 135, 136, 187
certified teachers 69, 185
Champagne Healing 76
chaos 60, 147, 176, 205
consciousness vii, 5, 8, 10, 13, 16, 20, 22, 25, 32, 38, 40, 55, 61, 64, 65, 67, 68, 69, 70, 83, 88, 102, 104, 110, 116, 118, 119, 129, 142, 143, 144, 145, 147, 148, 153, 155, 156, 157, 158, 160, 162, 164, 165, 166, 167, 168, 174, 191, 193, 205, 209, 211, 217, 219
Cosmic Battery 176, 177, 178, 179, 180

D
Dagmar 25, 27, 30, 34
David Bohm 153, 157
Deepak Chopra 7, 51, 224
DNA 20, 41, 42, 43, 46, 87, 152, 153, 154, 155, 156, 157, 158, 162, 166, 185, 200, 211, 220, 224
dragons 21, 22, 25, 33, 36, 200

E
eighth-dimensional 13
electrical connection 59
Element of Air 19
Element of Earth 14
Element of Fire 17
Element of Water 15
entrains 68

F
frequency 3, 8, 9, 52, 65, 66, 72, 85, 95, 109, 148, 150, 153, 159, 162, 163, 176, 225

G
Ggantija 46
Giorgio Gronget de Vasse 24
Glenda Green 5, 119, 224
God Consciousness 117, 167
Grail Codes 10, 20, 21, 22, 25, 26, 31, 33, 34, 37, 40, 41, 42, 152, 157, 158, 167, 200

H

Hawkins 142, 143, 144, 145, 220, 224
healing 6, 7, 9, 11, 12, 15, 54, 55, 60, 62, 69, 73, 83, 84, 86, 91, 93, 94, 104, 105, 107, 111, 114, 115, 116, 117, 118, 120, 121, 122, 123, 124, 127, 129, 131, 132, 138, 150, 160, 162, 166, 172, 176, 177, 181, 186, 187, 190, 191, 205, 206, 217
Himalayan Heart Activation 14, 171, 172, 173
holographic 65, 157, 210, 211, 212
Hubert Zeitlmair 26
Hypogeum 30

I

initiations 13, 16, 69, 166
Initiatory Gridwork 218
intention 14, 53, 54, 55, 66, 67, 68, 69, 70, 71, 73, 76, 87, 90, 91, 93, 94, 99, 100, 101, 103, 104, 108, 109, 113, 117, 123, 149, 154, 158, 159, 160, 161, 163, 173, 175, 181, 188, 189, 193, 207, 217, 218
Isis 35, 40, 43, 45, 200

J

John of God 116

K

karma 92, 188
Kilimanjaro 17, 18, 20, 46
kinesiology 141, 142, 143, 145, 147
Kurt Schildmann 27, 29

L

Lemuria 15, 211
Lightning Initiation 199, 211
Lobsang Rampa 212, 225

M

Machaelle Small Wright 58, 59
Malta 19, 20, 21, 22, 23, 24, 25, 26, 27, 28, 29, 30, 34, 36, 37, 45, 157, 200, 220
Map of Consciousness 141, 142, 143, 147
Mark vii, 3, 12, 13, 20, 21, 22, 32, 39, 49, 120, 154, 156, 164, 165, 166, 167, 168, 191, 193
McTaggart 159, 221, 225
mental disorders 61, 136
Michael Newton 51, 58
Mosta 23, 24, 25
multidimensional vii, 65, 83, 107, 153, 156, 163, 164, 165, 168, 171, 196, 197, 217, 218

N

Nepal 14, 15, 46, 171

P

permission 15, 45, 109
Peru 15, 18, 22, 23, 46, 166
Peter Moon 210, 220
Poseidon 34, 36, 37
pregnant 188
proto-Sanskrit 27, 34

Q

quantum 13, 65, 69, 91, 153, 155, 156, 157, 158, 159, 168, 195, 196
Quantum Field 156
Quetzalcoatl 16

R

Radu Cinamar 203, 207, 210, 211
Reiki 83, 104, 121, 122, 166
resonance 8, 66, 67, 68, 71, 85, 120, 156, 159, 161, 195
resonant field 68, 87, 92, 110

S

shaman 13, 15, 155, 201
sleeping goddess 30, 31, 42
Solar Grail 39, 42
Sphinx 43, 212, 213, 215
sun disc 15, 16, 23, 40, 41, 43
Sun Disc Codes 16, 17, 20, 22, 40

T

The Eagle and the Condor 17, 21
Transylvania 36, 203, 204, 207, 210, 213

V

Valerie Hunt 9, 163
vibrations 8, 9, 41, 52, 67, 95, 100, 151, 153, 162, 164, 166, 176, 179, 190, 196, 211, 218
visualization 87
Vladimir Poponin 155

W

White Eagle vii, 12, 14, 15, 17, 19, 25, 32, 39, 54, 57, 61, 83, 112, 174, 178, 181, 189, 199, 200, 208, 214, 218

Z

Zecharia Sitchin 35
Zeitlmair 25, 27, 28, 29, 30, 31, 34, 35, 36, 206

About the Author

Jonette Crowley is the creator of the Soul Body Fusion technique for healing and wholeness. She is an internationally respected spiritual teacher and founder of the Center for Creative Consciousness, an organization dedicated to spiritual awakening. Jonette is an explorer—both in the inner planes and in her travels around the world.

She is a modern-day mystic, with gifts of clairvoyance and healing, and the unique ability to hold energies that lift others to experience their own inner truths. Since the late 1980s she has received and shared the teachings of her spirit guides: White Eagle and Mark. With their guidance, Jonette teaches transformational workshops and retreats in the United States and Europe. She has traveled extensively—to over sixty countries—and now leads sacred adventure tours to power spots around the world. You can learn about trips, workshops, classes on the web, CDs and audio downloads, free meditations, and phone sessions with White Eagle at www.JonetteCrowley.com. And stay up to date on events and information on Soul Body Fusion at www.SoulBodyFusion.com.

Jonette is also firmly rooted in the corporate world. She has an MBA and holds the academic honor of Phi Beta Kappa. She and her husband, Ed Oakley, own a nationally known leadership consulting firm, Enlightened Leadership Solutions (see www.enleadership.com). She and Ed live in the suburbs of Denver, Colorado. They love skiing in the Rockies in the winter and hiking and golf in the summer. She has three adult stepchildren, a niece, and seven nephews.

Endnotes

1. Glenda Green, 88
2. Deepak Chopra, *Reinventing the Body, Resurrecting the Soul* 3
3. Manjir Samanta-Laughton, *Punk Science*, 139
4. Information compiled from www.MaltaDiscovery.org, www.philipcoppens.com/burrowscave, and "The Burrows Cave Enigma," http://www.bibliotecapleyades.net/sociopolitica/esp_sociopol_underground12.htm
5. Information on the Zeitlmairs' research compiled from www.MaltaDiscovery.org
6. Michael Newton, *Destiny of Souls*, 111
7. Ibid., 113
8. Ibid., 8-9
9. Richard Gerber in Eric Pearl, *The Reconnection*, 211
10. Green, *Love Without End*, 14
11. Ibid., 15
12. David Hawkins, *Power vs. Force*, 70
13. Ibid., 85
14. Ibid., 219
15. Bruce Lipton, *The Biology of Belief*, throughout. See especially the chapter "It's the Environment, Stupid."
16. Ibid., 61
17. Lee Carroll (Kryon), *The Twelve Layers of DNA*, Book 12, 111
18. Grazyna Fosar and Franz Bludorf, "DNA can be influenced and reprogrammed by words and frequencies: Russian DNA Discoveries," http://www.soulsofdistortion.nl/dna1.html
19. Ibid.

20 Carroll (Kryon), Book 12. 16
21 Craig Hamilton, "The Self-Aware Universe: An Interview with Amit Goswami" [Abridged], http://twm.co.nz/goswam1.htm
22 Lynne McTaggart, *The Intention Experiment*, xxix
23 Wayne Dyer, *The Power of Intention*, 9
24 Marco Bischof, "What are Biophotons?" www.marcobischof.com/en/arbeitsgebiete/biophotonen.html
25 Stephen Linsteadt, "Frequency Fields at the Cellular Level," http://www.naturalhealinghouse.com/frequency.htm
26 Sanaya Roman and Duane Packer, "What Is the Light Body?" www.orindaben.com/pages/light_body/abtlb111_6/#03what www.orindaben.com
27 T. Lobsang Rampa, *The Cave of the Ancients*, 83
28 Ibid., 84-85, 92